I0753305

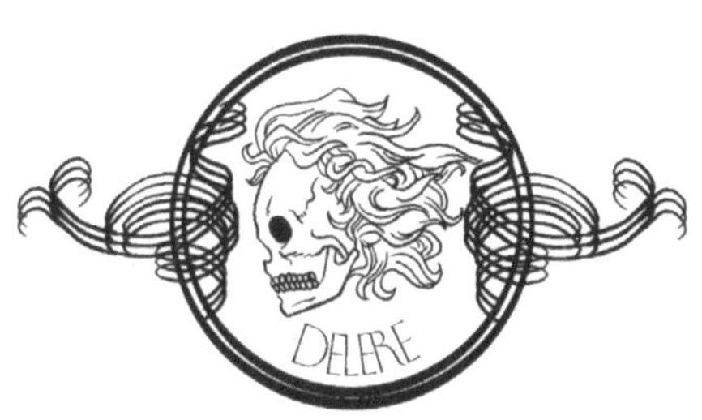
DELERE

THIS PAPERBACK EDITION 1ST PUBLISHED IN 2017 BY DELERE PRESS LLP

*   *   *

FIRST PUBLISHED IN 2017 BY DELERE PRESS LLP
BLOCK 370G ALEXANDRA ROAD
#09-09 SINGAPORE 159960
WWW.DELEREPRESS.COM
DELERE PRESS LLP REG NO. T11LL1061K

ISBN 978-981-11-3087-8

WHY HASN'T JB ALREADY DISAPPEARED

DELERE PRESS

Layout design by Yanyun Chen
Cover image by Untitled, Zusammenkunft I © Grace Euna Kim, 2015

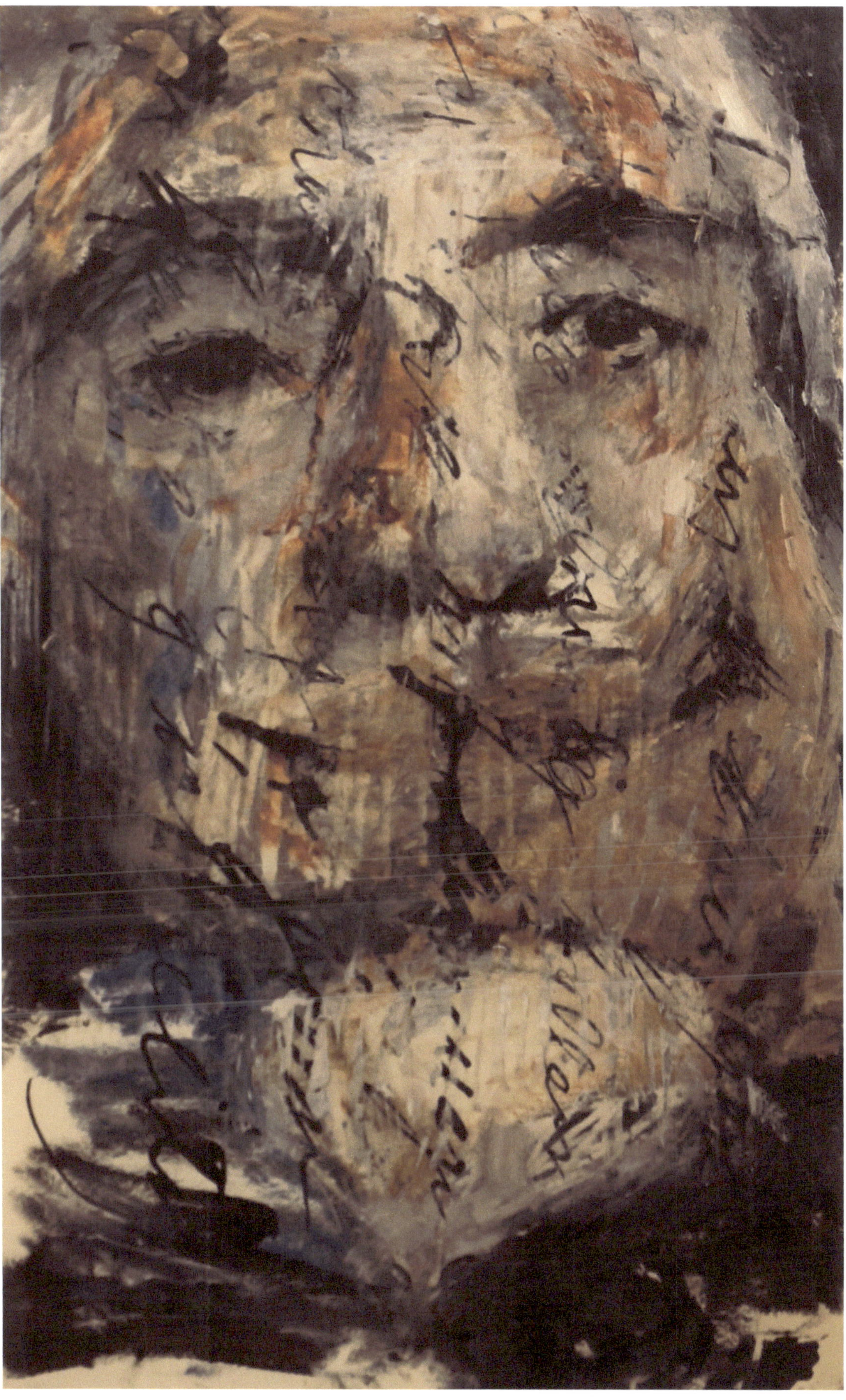

White on white translucent black capes
Back on the rack
Bela Lugosi's dead
The bats have left the bell tower
The victims have been bled
Red velvet lines the black box
Bela Lugosi's dead
Bela Lugosi's dead
Undead undead undead
Undead undead undead

LES ENTRETIENS IMPOSSIBLES

TRADUIT PAR DANIEL KWANG GUAN CHAN

Alors que nous avons cette conversation, alors que je parle avec — peut-être même à — toi, alors que tu m'écoutes peut-être ou même que tu prêtes attention à ce *parler*-ci [*here-speak*], je me demande [*wonder*] — ou je pourrais errer [*wander*] avec de la question — s'il est même possible de parler de la mort ;

sans mentionner, parler *à* la Mort : elle-même
lui-même
soi-même

Car, alors même que nous passons beaucoup de notre temps à raconter des histoires de la mort, de morts, sur les morts qui ne sont pas seulement des morts, nous ne faisons que des énoncés au sujet de la mort, peut-être même des énoncés décrivant des morts, mais nous ne sommes jamais vraiment capable de dire ce qu'est la mort ;

et encore moins qui.

Ce qui ouvre la question : parle-t-on des morts
ou, de l'idée de ceux qui sont morts

Gardant à l'esprit que la mort — ou la Mort, si tu préfères les noms propres — reste au-delà de nous. La mort, c'est quelque chose qu'on éprouve ; et à ma connaisance, personne n'est revenu pour nous dire à qui nous faisons face, à quoi nous faisons face. Ou, à qui l'on fait face, car l'on fait peut-être toujours face à la mort seul.

Même le nazaréen.

Tout ce qu'il a fait était : annoncer sa resurrection, nous dire que *pour vaincre la mort, il suffit de mourir*. Cependant, il n'a pas pris la peine de nous dire exactement qui — ou ce qu' — il a conquis.

Ce qui, en soi, n'est pas une raison de douter de ses paroles, sa preténtion.

Peut-être qu'il a bien surmonté l'idée de la mort — mais a laissé ses effets intacts. Après tout, la derniere fois que j'ai vérifié, les gens étaient encore affectés, encore en train de mourir.

Pour ça je suis — aussi morbide que cela puisse paraître — étrangement reconnaissant. Ainsi, je sais au moins que je parle avec toi.

Ou, au moins avec la possibilité de toi.

Mais quel toi ?

Car, il faut essayer de ne pas oublier,
que tout le monde meurt deux fois — une fois corporellement ;
l'autre fois quand on est oublié.

Ce qui pourrait aussi signifier qu'il y a deux — il y a plus d'un — *toi*. Que parler avec l'un d'entre eux implique la mort d'un autre *toi* ; tous les autres *toi*. Et que, puisque je te parle — du moins puisque j'essaie de le faire — cela signifie que même les *toi* non-morts doivent être morts.

Ainsi, je ne peux parler avec toi qu'en mémoire de toi.

Car, alors que je fais appel à toi
t'appelle
dis que tu es mort
suis en mesure d'écrire sur toi seulement parce que tu es mort
tu es mort parce que j'écris sur toi.

mon seul accès à toi est à travers ton nom ; tout ce dont je parle, tout ce que je peux prononcer, est ton nom.

Ainsi, tous les essais — tout ce que je peux essayer de faire est — de parler de toi, à toi, imaginativement. Et ici, il faut garder à l'esprit que l'imagination naît de la mémoire : parce que pour imaginer quelque chose, pour en avoir une petite idée, il faut d'abord en savoir quelque chose.

Mais, de la mort, je ne sais rien
ne peux rien savoir

Or, nous continuons à parler des morts
je continue à parler de toi

Ainsi, à parler toujours et déjà de l'indicible
Ou, peut-être : un discours d'un souvenir que je n'ai pas encore.

Et, puisque la mort est probablement un souvenir à venir — même si tu ne m'avais jamais quitté — alors peut-être que le seul moyen pour moi, pour nous, d'en savoir quelque chose, c'est d'être toujours déjà mort ; et d'être en attente que nos corps rattrapent ce souvenir, ce souvenir de l'inconnu.

Peut-être alors, en parlant de la mort elle parle à travers moi
en te parlant tu parles à travers moi

— dans un entretien infini —

dans lequel , parler de toi est toujours aussi un essai d'être en communion avec les morts, peut-être même avec la Mort elle-même. Et, dans lequel la Mort n'est rien de plus qu'un nom ; qui ne nomme rien, sauf le fait qu'il nomme :

une dénomination qui — se réalise à travers soi
est toujours déjà aussi au-delà de soi
est en dehors de soi

ainsi, toujours déjà, en extase ;
dans une extase de la communication

mais qui
te nomme peut-être ...

EN ATTENDANT JB ...

When I am gone,
all I want is to disappear … so
why are they still
talking about me …

— JB

Theonewhocalledforadisappearance even before he disappeared. Perhaps the one who disappeared when he was with us; and now that he is gone, has played the final trick — has had the last laugh — not by returning, resurrecting, but by completely disappearing.

Thus ensuring that he will always haunt us.

And here, we should perhaps tune our registers to the spectres that haunt haunting itself: for, a haunt is both familiar, a place of comfort, a place we go to hang out with our friends, and foreign, unknown, potentially frightening. And what is more familiar, and unknowable, than death itself: it is both always already in us, and always also to come. For, the moment we are named, the moment our names come to us, is also the moment when we are anointed with the utterance that is left behind after us. And since names only come into being when they are uttered, each time our name is called is also a preparation for the moment when there is nothing to call but our name.

This is the peril of friendship.

For, as Jacques Derrida reminds us, « to have a friend, to look at him, to follow him with your eyes, to admire him in friendship, is to know in a more intense way, already injured, always insistent, and more and more unforgettable, that one of the two of you will inevitably see the other die ».[1]

And, it is precisely this that JB pre-empts; for, he claims: « the whole art is to know how to disappear before dying and instead of dying ».[2] The trouble though, he continues, is that « nothing just vanishes; of everything that disappears there remains traces. The problem is what remains when everything has disappeared. It's a bit like Lewis Carroll's Cheshire Cat, whose grin still hovers in the air after the rest of him has vanished ... Now, a cat's grin is already something terrifying, but the grin without the cat is something even more terrifying ... ».[3] Clearly, the irony of the situation is not lost on JB: after all, the title of the text — *Why Hasn't Everything Already Disappeared?* — comes in the form of a question, doesn't purport to give any answers, is a question that maintains itself as a question even whilst playing at answering. In fact, it is a questioning of a question, of all questions. And as one is reading it, how can one not smile?

Grin.

...

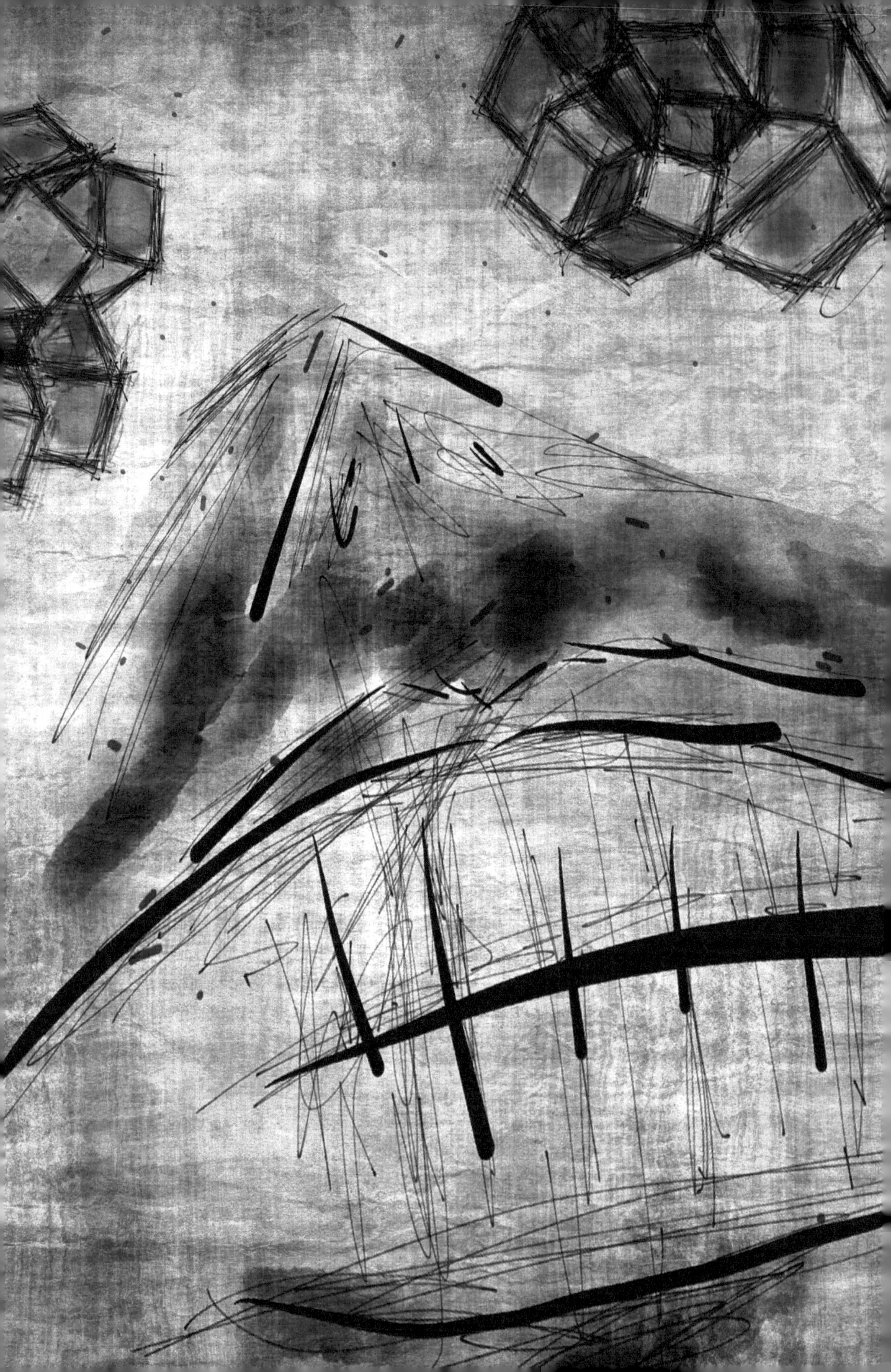

There was a time when a smile was much harder to muster.

How to still smile?

But, what else can one do but smile?

7 March 2007.
3am.
A text message from Tombie Rautenbach.

« Baudrillard is dead »

For, as Marine Dupius tells Wolfgang Schirmacher, « when I asked why he was smiling, he replied, 'what else can I do ...' ».

Perhaps it is his smile that remains.

A smile that remains with us even when he is gone ... a smile without a person ... a smile that terrifies us. For, even as we gaze upon the smile, even as a smile breaks out on our faces (and here, we should never forget that often-times we cannot control when we smile; it happens to us, infects us, takes over), we have no idea why we are smiling. And there is nothing more terrifying than a mystery, a secret.

mysterium tremendum.

But even as we potentially tremble, we should also retune our receptors to the track in *The Transparency of Evil* where he teaches us of the evils of complete transparency, which would be the point where « every individual category is subject to contamination, substitution is possible between any sphere and any other: there is total confusion of types ».[4] At that juncture, « each category is generalized to the greatest possible extent, so that it eventually loses all specificity and is reabsorbed by all the other categories. When everything is political, nothing is political anymore, the word itself is meaningless. When everything is sexual, nothing is sexual anymore, and sex loses its determinants. When everything is aesthetic, nothing is beautiful or ugly anymore, and art itself disappears. This paradoxical state of affairs, which is simultaneously the complete actualization of an idea, the perfect realization of the whole tendency of modernity, and the negation of the idea and that tendency, their annihilation by virtue of their very success, by virtue of their extension beyond their own bounds ... ».[5] Perhaps then, in any notion, idea, thought, what remains crucial is its own, its very, limits — boundaries, borders.

Exteriority. Which suggests that for any thinking to be singular, there has to be something that remains external to it. For thinking to mean something — even if we constitute meaning as the significance of something rather than its signification — it has to have an outside; something must remain beyond it, outside of it.

Where, it is what remains outside, always already there and also beyond us, that continues to haunt all thought. This is the spectre in thinking that Werner Hamacher never lets us forget: in all attempts to think, « understanding is in want of understanding ».[6] So, even as we attempt to understand, to know, to touch the beyond, the other, we have to open our receptors to Avital Ronell's crossed-line, open a connection to her teaching, and keep in mind the notion that « the connection to the other is a reading — not an interpretation, assimilation, or even a hermeneutic understanding, but a reading ».[7] And if each connection is a reading, it brings with it all the blindness inherent in reading: not a blindness that is an antonym to seeing, but a blindness in sight itself. For, not only can we not know if what we are reading is of, is from, the text — even if we are attempting to read in full fidelity to the text, we can only test our reading after reading — each time we read, we have to first assume the very possibility of reading itself. In other words — and here, what choice have we but to use the words of the other — we can never know if each reading is also quite possibly a rewriting of the other, of the very thing we are attempting to read, of reading itself. Thus, each reading is always already fraught with the potential impossibility of reading. But, it would be silly to claim that reading doesn't change us: it affects us, has effects on us. Which suggests that reading occurs in spite of its impossibility. Perhaps then, all we can say is that each time we read, we are reading *as if* we can read. This is reading not as an act (otherwise its *impotentiality not-to-be* would be effaced), but as an event: reading as nothing but the openness to the possibility of reading. How it occurs, and the manner in which it affects us though, potentially remains secret from us — where, even as we may be reading, we remain completely blind to it.[8]

Thinking …

— reading; or, what remains to be read —

… or what is to be thought.

And perhaps,
this is what truly
makes us tremble.

If we are unable to know what moves us, let alone why, this suggests that this is an affectation that comes from elsewhere; a change that occurs, but one which our senses may not be privy to. Thus, each reading is quite possibly a *trans-substantiation*. Which suggests that each change is one that is affected by another, even if this other potentially remains veiled from us. And here, if we pay attention, we can hear echoes of the ones who have opened registers in us, altered our beings, perhaps even ruptured us — teachers, teachings. The fact that I am evoking my teachers — Avital Ronell, Werner Hamacher, Wolfgang Schirmacher, JB — should not be lost on us, especially if we allow Martin Heidegger's teaching to resound. For, he teaches: « teaching is even more difficult that learning ... because what teaching calls for is this: to let learn. The real teacher, in fact, lets nothing else be learned than — learning. The teacher is far ahead of his apprentices in this alone, that he has still far more to learn than they — he has to learn to let them learn ... The teacher is far less assured of his ground than those who learn are of theirs ».[9] And, this might just be why the only one who can write is not the one teaching but the one who is taught. For, as one writes, even if one is writing in an attempt to respond, in openness to possibilities, one has no choice but to make a statement, no matter how provisional; and in that moment, one is staking a claim, making a stand, grounding where there is no *grund*.

... the highest function of the sign is to make reality disappear and, at the same time, to mask that disappearance ...

— JB, Crime Parfait

For, as I am attempting to write, to resound with teachings, teachers, as I write, there is no way to verify not only if my writing is an echo, or if I am rewriting. More pertinently, there is no way to even know if I have been taught. So, as I write, I am always also writhing, sliding, slipping, attempting to capture a teaching, whilst trying to evade accusations of being a *dilettante*, of not learning, being a bad student, or even of betraying the very teachers I am attempting to attend to, respond with.

And, even as I attempt to be faithful to those teachings by citing, quoting — *trying to let JB speak for himself,* as it were — each homage is fraught with the possibility that even though these are his words, they are also not his; not just because of the potential mis-attributions that haunt all citations, but — more importantly — that even if these are his words, they are always out of context. This would be the very violence that is enacted on him, and his memory: each attempt to preserve his words is also a murder of his very words, his very thought. It is no coincidence that quotation marks are sometimes referred to as vampire marks — not only are we dealing with the undead as we murder to resurrect, we are also sucking the very life out of the words we quote. For, as we cite someone, we are staking our claim on her, driving our stake through her. And, whilst enacting this murder, we are also putting our stakes down on them, betting on not only the notion that we might be defending our position through them, shielding ourselves with their name(s) (as if to say, if you disagree with me, take it up with JB), but also gambling on the premise that no one will notice that we are hiding behind phantoms;

prosopopoeia

In her wonderful reading of the relationality between Goethe and Eckermann in *Dictations*, Avital Ronell unveils the tension that lies in all biography — between writing on, about, and re-writing: « ... by announcing, 'this is *my* Goethe' he is immunizing his enterprise against any possible contestation that might be brought to bear on this text. In asserting a part of Goethe that is wholly his own, namely Eckermann's, he renders this work invulnerable to attack ... he establishes the status of the text as testimony and, as such, the only criteria for truth must be derived from the purely subjective effect that Goethe produced on Eckermann ... As object of testimony, Goethe will remain mysterious, elusive and safe from any attempt to pin him down ... If this is *his* Goethe we cannot properly have any access to him; and if, then, Goethe is unknowable as a total object of any discourse, then Eckermann is also at the very beginning disclaiming any possibility for representing the true Goethe. Yet in saying 'this is my Goethe, this facet of Goethe is the reflection that I perceive' he is claiming to disclose precisely that facet of Goethe which is the only image or manifestation of Goethe to which one can ever hope to accede. Eckermann's project is therefore, from the start, or before and after the start — that is, in the preface, already entangled in contradiction ».[10] And here, it might be helpful to turn again to Werner Hamacher, and tune our dials to his teaching that « ellipsis is the rhetorical equivalent of writing: it depletes, or de-completes, the whole so as to make conceptual totalities possible. And yet every conceivable whole achieved on the basis of ellipsis is stamped with the mark of the original loss. Like writing, it withdraws from the alternatives of presence and absence, whole and part, proper and foreign, because only on its ever eroding foundation can conceptual oppositions develop: it withdraws from its own concept. Ellipsis eclipses (itself). It is the 'figure' of figuration: the area no figure contains ... ».[11] And, since the ellipsis is « the 'figure' of figuration, the area no figure contains », this suggests that each sentence quite possibly contains an ellipsis — whether we see it or not is perhaps irrelevant. In fact, it is precisely the ellipsis that allows writing to occur — for, if there were ever a complete, total, sentence, it would never have to be written again. We can only continue writing due to the possibility of the incompleteness of the sentence. Even if exactly the same sentence.

The ellipsis ...
what both allows writing, and
ensures that we will always be
writhing as we write ...

My JB ... held ... together ... apart ...   by the ellipsis.

More than that ... JB ... always already elliptical ...

...

At this point, we might take a little segue and adjust our dials to an apparently unrelated register, tune in to the fact that the text Ronell was commenting on, speaking with — *Conversations* — is a text that registers the attempts of Eckermann to speak with his master, Goethe. For, this is also an attempt at conversing; even as I am writing JB, quite possibly narrating a tale about a JB that has naught to do with him, I am also attempting to converse with, respond to, him, with and through other teachers, masters. And here, if one is slightly generous, one might notice that the ellipsis bears resemblances to, echoes of, the telephone.

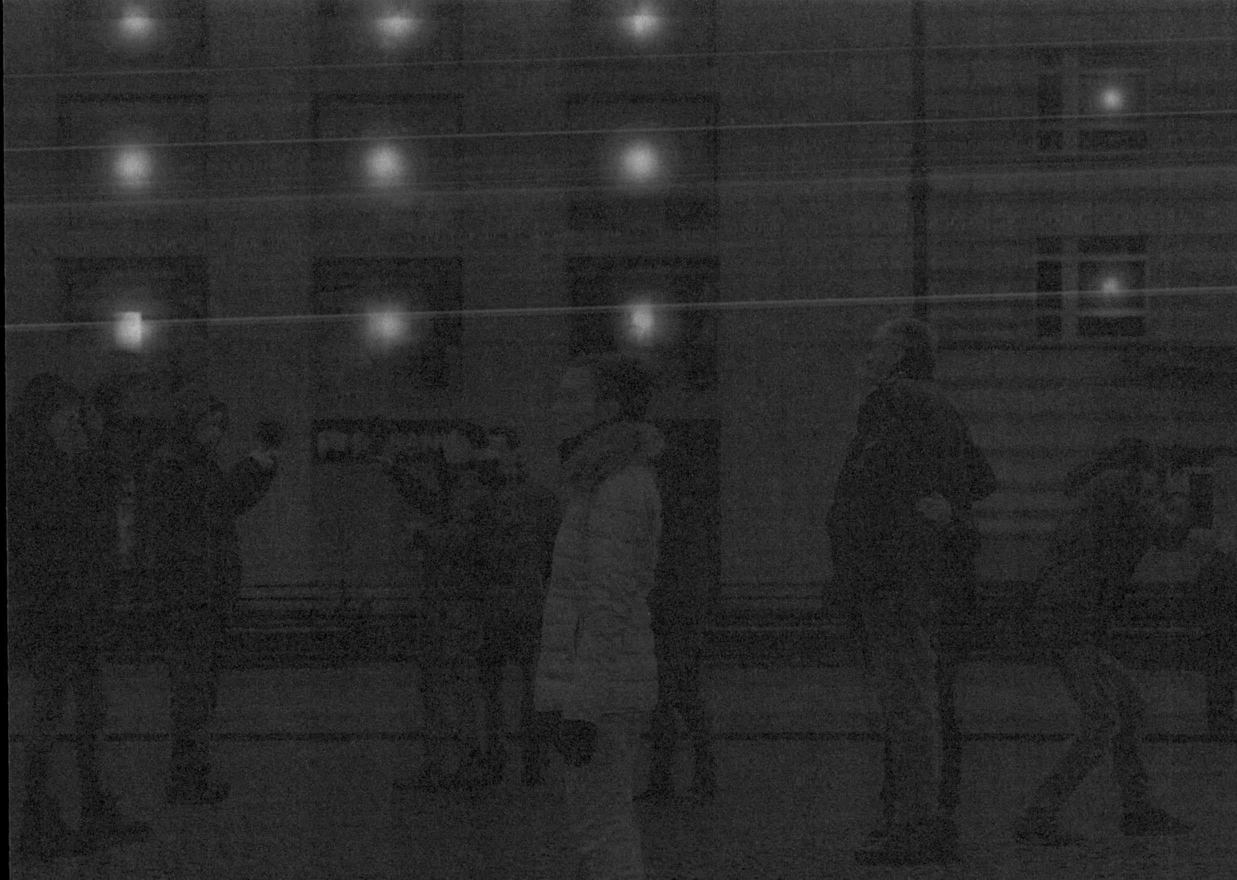

Dial tone:

... pulse phone ... dialing for a pulse ...

Perhaps it is only these searching pulses, these tones, which prevent us from leaping over — completely — into death. After all, a sentence is often difficult, if not impossible, to repeal. And if *graphien*, as Jacques Derrida maintains, is on the side of death, what maintains life, *bios*, is perhaps the unknowability that continues to beep. [Here, we should not forget Giorgio Agamben's claim that the Greeks distinguished between one's bare life, and one's political life — one's *zoë* from one's *bios*. And if we follow this trace a little more, we cannot ignore the fact that the account of one's life is called one's biography — the writing of one's *bios*. Hence, the life that is being attended to is the one that concerns the *polis*, one's relation with the community; one's symbolic life. One's real life, bodily life, remains veiled, secret; quite possibly even from oneself, from one's self.][12]

We should also try not to forget the pact made between Alexander Graham Bell and his brother Melville whilst working on an early prototype of the telephone: whomever died first was to try and make contact with the other. What the other had to do was: listen for the other's call. And pick up the phone.

... Ring ...[13]

I must note it right here, on the morning of 22 August 1979, 10 A.M., while typing this page for publication, the telephone rings. The U.S. The American operator asks me if I accept a 'collect call' from Martin (she says Martine or martini) Heidegger. I heard, as one often does in these situations which are very familiar to me, often having to call "collect" myself, voices that I thought I recognised on the other end of the intercontinental line, listening to me and watching my reaction. What will he do with the ghost or Geist of Martin? I cannot summarise here all the chemistry of the calculation that very quickly made me refuse ("It's a joke, I do not accept") after having the name Martini Heidegger repeated several times, hoping that the author of the farce would finally name himself. Who pays, in sum, the addressee or the sender? who is to pay? This is a very difficult question, but this morning I thought, I should not pay, at least not otherwise than by adding this note of thanks.

— Jacques Derrida,
La Carte Postale

Not that we can ever know what we will hear when we pick up. For, even in this day of caller-identification-technology, one never really knows who, if anyone, is on the other side until we lift the receiver to our ears. Hence, there is always a risk that comes with attempting to respond: who hasn't had their day ruined by a bad phone call. Thus, each time we open ourselves to responding, each time we open ourselves to an unknown other, we are also putting our very self on the line.

Where, even if one doesn't pick up — doesn't accept — the call, one is quite possibly already affected, wounded; without even, or ever, knowing by whom, let alone why.

And even if a conversation ensues, we might never be certain what we are speaking about, on; let alone whom we are speaking to. Perhaps all we can ever know, as Maurice Blanchot beautifully posits in *L'attente l'oubli*, is « perhaps she was speaking ... ».[14] For, one can only pick up on a sound after it happens; but even as the sound resounds in one, one might never quite be able to know why. And even though one can try to guess, take a position, each attempt to attend to a possibility entails a reading of the sound, a sound that has passed, happened, a speaking that « was ». This is an attending in the present to an event that has passed, or perhaps an event that is only to come. Hence, all one can do is attend to — await — the potential conversation.

Not that there is any object — even less so an objective — to this waiting: for, « as soon as one waited for something, one waited a little less ».[15] After all, to wait is « to make oneself attentive to that which makes of waiting a neutral act, coiled upon itself in tight circles, the innermost and outermost of which would coincide, attention distracted in waiting and returned all the way to the unexpected. Waiting, waiting that is the refusal to wait for anything ... ».[16] For, this is a waiting that does not claim to understand waiting; is quite possibly a « waiting and without waiting ».[17] However, just because one cannot know does not alleviate one's responsibility: for, one must continue to attend, to pay attention; « and the essence of attention is the ability to preserve, in and through itself, that which is always on this side of attention and the source of all waiting: mystery. Attention, the welcoming of that which escapes attention, an opening onto the unexpected, waiting that is the unexpected in all waiting ».[18] One waits, attends, even though there may well be nothing that one is attending to, waiting for — after all, « only waiting gives attention. Empty time, with no project, is waiting that gives attention ... Waiting gives attention while withdrawing everything that is awaited ».[19] Thus, each time we speak, attempt to speak, we are always putting forth not only a response to someone else, but also awaiting — not for something, someone; just waiting.

Where perhaps, what is essential to conversation is nothing other than — waiting.

And, this is perhaps why Blanchot could have only begun with: « Here, and on this sentence that was perhaps also meant for him, he was obliged to stop ».[20] Herein lies the mystery, the secret: « the secret — what a crude word — was nothing other than the fact that she spoke and deferred speaking ».[21] And this is precisely what makes him, us, tremble — the fact that she, all conversation, is speaking and not speaking; waiting for nothing but the possibility of speaking. By attempting to converse with her — whomever her is, was — he had, has, opened himself to nothing but waiting.

And, all he could do from then on was to be

awaiting oblivion.

...

Whoever said it would be easy?

Sometimes to smile, you just have to — as the saying goes — *grin and bear it*.

People say I'm the life of the party
'cause I tell a joke or two
Although I might be laughing loud and hearty
Deep inside I'm blue
So take a good look at my face
You'll see my smile looks out of place
If you look closer, it's easy to trace
The tracks of my tears ...

— Smokey Robinson & The Miracles

•••

And, even as I say « my JB » one should try to recall what Søren Kierkegaard never lets us forget: « 'My' — what does the word designate? Not what belongs to me, but what I belong to, what contains my whole being, which is mine insofar as I belong to it ».[22] This is also the lesson Avital Ronell leaves us with: it is not so much that Goethe dictates, dictates to, Eckermann, nor that Eckermann is effacing Goethe; *Conversations* is Eckermann-Goethe. For, whenever we attempt to converse, the moment we pick up the telephone, we are always already in communion; with all the mysteries of *trans-substantiation* haunting us. Goethe is immortalised through writing: not just his own writing, or the writing of Eckermann (or anyone who writes on, about, of, him), but in writing itself. For, in writing, inscribing, one is always already immortalising, precisely by being in, with, the order of death. As Tim Rice and Andrew Lloyd-Webber so eloquently posit in *Jesus Christ Superstar*, « to conquer death, you only have to die ... ». And here, one should bear in mind that immortality and death have an intimate relationship — one cannot be immortal unless one has passed over to, into, the side of death. However, just because they are in a relationality does not mean they are the same. Like Eckermann-Goethe, immortality-death are always already touching yet separated — by a dash. And it is precisely, quite possibly only, this dash — gap — that allows them to converse in the first place. For, if they were in the same place, space, all possibility of communication would be destroyed, effaced: after all, as Jean-Luc Nancy teaches us, « there can only be relation ... if we start with an absolute distancing, without which there would be no possibility of proximity, of identity or strangeness, of subjectivity or thinghood ».[23]

For, it is space that one first needs in order to touch.

My —

perhaps he is only mine not just insofar as I am his but more radically because he is no longer mine. For, I can only make any claim to him, about him, insofar as that claim remains stable, dead. Each time I speak, write, about him, I invoke his name, keeping in mind that each name is *catachrestic*; naming nothing but the fact that it is naming. Every invocation — allowing all the echoes of necromancy to resound here — calls forth one name whilst ignoring all the other potential names. Perhaps that is precisely what is radical about names: at the root, *en route* even, they do nothing but prepare for the inevitability of one's absence — the point where one becomes other to oneself, an illusion of one's self. But it is not as if JB doesn't already know this. In fact, this is his radicality, his very own radical alterity: « It is all in the art of disappearing. Only that which arrives in the mode of disappearance is truly other. But this disappearance must leave a trace, even the place where the Other, the world or the object appeared. It is in fact the only way for the Other to exist: through your disappearance. 'We shall be your favourite disappearing act!' »[24] By writing about JB, we are not preventing his disappearance: this is not some nostalgic act of keeping him with us, recalling him, refusing his disappearance.

This is writing so he can disappear;
writing his disappearance.

Not just writing his radical alterity.
But, writing as radical alterity.

For, it is not just that writing is on the side of death, but more radically that each writing is always already the writing of another, the other: this is a disappearance through illusion; keeping in mind that « illusion is not opposed to reality, it is another, more subtle reality that envelops the first with the sign of its disappearance ».[25] This is a disappearance through multiplication. By letting himself be anything you want him to be, by allowing you to believe that he will always be with you, he has already slipped past.

Disappearance through seduction;
your seduction: « for behind the only existing form of immortality, that of artifice, there lies the idea incarnated in the stars, that death itself shines by its absence, that death can be turned into a brilliant and superficial appearance, that it is itself a seductive surface ... ».[26]

Writing as I have been seduced ...

When I passed you in the doorway,
You took me with a glance
Should have took that last bus home
But I asked you for a dance

— Thin Lizzy

... not like there was anything I could do about it.

• • •

Whoever said one will always like one's lessons.

For, teaching one a lesson often involves a beating, sometimes brutal. And, learning — opening a new register — entails an act of violence. Which potentially comes with, brings with it, rupture, splitting, wounding.

Trauma

And here, one should try to bear in mind Plato's warning that even as philosophy and poetry are the highest arts, forms of thinking, they can also potentially destroy you.

• • •

Fne can only be seduced by another, an other that remains completely other, radically other — an enigma.

In other words, an object.

And not an object in the sense that we say *object of desire*; for, that would presume a certain accessibility — and, even if we were not certain, could never be certain, why that particular object called out to us, there would still be a notion, at least momentarily, of what this object is, was. This is an object in the most radical sense of the word: something that remains before one (*ob* 'against', *jacere* 'to throw'); where, in remaining before one, there has to be a gap between one's self and the object (to throw entails a particular involvement, contact; which implies both an initial and eventual distance between the object and one). This is an object that remains before us to remind us of the fact that there is always already space between our self and itself: it is a mass. And here, one must not forget JB's warning: « the term 'mass' is not a concept. It is a leitmotif of political demagogy, a soft, sticky, lumpen-analytical notion. A good sociology would attempt to surpass it with 'more subtle' categories: socio-professional ones, categories of class, cultural status, etc. This is wrong: it is by prowling around these soft and acritical notions (like 'mana' once was) that one can go further than intelligent critical sociology. Besides, it will be noticed retrospectively that the concepts 'class,' 'social relations,' 'power,' 'status,' 'institution,' and 'social' itself — all these too explicit concepts which are the glory of the legitimate sciences — have also only ever been muddled notions themselves, but notions upon which agreement has nevertheless been reached for mysterious ends: those of preserving a certain code of analysis ... To want to specify the term 'mass' is a mistake — it is to provide meaning for that which has none ».[27] To claim to understand the other — to put it back under meaning — is the same mistake; it is to provide meaning for that which has none.

One is seduced because one is seduced.

One should never pretend to know,
nor pretend to be an expert.

One should always remain an amateur.

For, this is also the very juncture of love. Where, even as love is an openness to another — an other that remains whole in her or him self, wholly other — there has to be a moment when one can also say that the other is yours. This is the very violence inherent in love: when one utters the phrase *I love you,* one is selecting one from every other. More than that, one is inflicting this selection regardless of the will of the other person: for, each utterance happens at a singular moment, one in which the feeling of the other remains beyond one's scope of knowing. At the moment of the utterance, one is completely blind to the other.

Where, in saying « my », the other person is — to one — an object, is one's object; even if, regardless of whether, the other objects to being one.

However, in being seduced, one also draws the seducer into the game. For, it takes two to tango. And, in writing on — about — another, one is also always already being written. Thus, not only is the object of one's writing on the side of death, so is the one that is allegedly writing.

Death — writhing — writing — death.

A truly fatal strategy.

• • •

In writing on JB, in writing his disappearance,
what else can I do but smile ...

...Grin.

It is our followers,
those who call themselves
our fellows, who we must truly be
wary of …

— JB

when one loos
one gains one

Translating one
Philosopher into another...
And another

Everybody,
participaiting
in the festival...

The
system itself
has no ___ limits.

ART! involves waste of TIME

The economy
of the waste

SIMULACRUM
Exchanged for
waste - profitability

Power!
floating... like money,
or language, or theory.

There are so much
information,
for such a short -
or even lack - of
information...

As soon as
you introduce death -
Death, as metaphor,
...

You can not think,
if you do not confront
Death

The real - no longer real - hyperreal,
US.
Desert cities - jungles of signs $

US, where only the wind
still plays... sand.

"ALL CONTENTS OF MEANING ARE ABSORBED I
FORM OF THE MEDIUM. ONLY THE
AN EVENT.

s everything,
words...

one looses faith,
or face?

Capitalism
has NO
face...

said the man,
who's death was
the only performance

well, they say...
one never looses
faith. when one
does not have one

LANGUAGE REMAINING
in PIECES...

...ing has been...
frozen. the museum
is everywhere!

"There is no better aphrodisiac, than innocence in
some grown-up eyes..."

...WHAT CAN
COME AFTER...?

"The sad thing about
artificial inteligence, is that
it lacks artifice - and therefore,
inteligence...

...Art, in this desert,
is everywhere, silence.

A reality without
origin - or a real
dissolving itsel into
ghosts...

visible past -
visible search -
the hope for new meanings...

Jean Baudrillard

THE ONLY DOMINANT
MEDIUM CAN MAKE

DREAMS OF HOPE

But what could art possibly mean in a world that has already become hyperrealist, cool, transparent, marketable? All it can do is make a final, paradoxical wink — the wink of reality laughing at itself in its most hyperrealist form … irony.

Yet this irony itself is no longer part of the accursed share. It now belongs to insider trading, the shameful and hidden complicity binding the artist who uses his or her aura of derision against the bewildered and doubtful masses.

Irony is also part of the conspiracy of art.

... and what hope have we when irony has been taken from us?

For, what else is irony but a gap — a space-between. And what else is space but the very condition of art itself; — space — which opens the possibility for us to be

living with art.

Not just material space, the space of materiality.

But that of imagination; the very place of possibilities.

The space for the work to be — maybe even to breathe.
Not in the way in which one wants, you want, it to be, but in the manner in which it is. And perhaps, at some point, if you are quiet enough, attentive enough — if one opens oneself to the work — it might whisper to you.

Might call out to you.
Which means that one's role — your choice — is to either pick up or not.

Not that one can ever know if one is answering a call from another, from the work, or if all one is hearing, if all you hear, are merely *voices in your head* ...

Which suggests that one cannot quite know what it says to one — nor, if it is even saying anything to one — at least with any certainty.

Why is the call thought of as something which, rather than taken, taken down, or taken in — be it from a specific agent, subject, principle, preferably a moral one — will be *given*? And if each call which issues is destined to make demands on the one who is called (but this is also questionable), is it already settled that I will hear, that I will hear this call and hear it as one destined for me? Is it not rather the case that the minimal condition to be able to hear something as something lies in my comprehending it neither as destined for me nor as somehow oriented toward someone else? Because I would not need to hear it in the first place if the source and destination of the call, of the call as call, were already certain and determined. Following the logic of calling up, of the call ... and along with that the logic of demand, of obligation, of law, no call can reach its addressee simply as itself, and each hearing is consummated in the realm of the possibility not so much of hearing as being able to listen up by ceasing to hear. Hearing ceases. It listens to a noise, a sound, a call; and so hearing always ceases hearing, because it could not let itself be determined other than as hearing, to hearing any further. Hearing ceases. Always. Listen ...

— Werner Hamacher

And here, what has to be resisted is the attempt to explain, to rationalise; to put whatever what thinks one might have heard — from the call — back under one's schema, schematics, heuristics, back under rationality itself. For, it is often easier to cling onto reason — no matter how fictive — than to not have anything to rely on. Which might be why conspiracy theories are so popular: underlying them is the logic that someone is in control; no matter how implausible this may be. Whether the reasons given are true or not are perhaps irrelevant: the fact of there being a reason, a cause, is better than if there were none. In many ways, it is even better if the reason were fictional: for, if grounded in a certain fact, or reality, it can then go away. However, if it were in the realm of the imagination, it is then always already possibly independent from materiality; thus, can be applied to any and every situation. And it is this, to echo Friedrich Nietzsche, that gives us us the *metaphysical comfort* that we can know — can dream we know — what is going on.

But to do so is to do nothing other than to break the relationality, the connection — to close all possibilities of the call itself. For, if subsumed, comprehended, it is also seized, grasped, apprehended; quite possibility torn apart.

And here, one should never forget — or at least try never to forget — the teaching of Jean Baudrillard: explication, attempts to explain, analysis, only break apart [*ana* 'up, throughout' + *lysis* 'a loosening,' from *lyein* 'to unfasten']. And, if beauty is of the order of the whole, the complete — even if this remains in the imaginary, as an idea, in the realm of the *eidos* — any attempt to analyse can only, at least might only, worsen. For art, like

the poem, lacks nothing: any commentary makes it worse. Not only does it lack nothing, but it makes any other discourse look superfluous.

... where grace is concerned, it is impossible for man to come anywhere near a puppet. Only a god can equal inanimate matter in this respect.

Grace appears most purely in that human form which either has no consciousness or an infinite consciousness. That is, in the puppet or in the god ...

— Heinrich von Kleist

However,
it is not as if opening oneself to the possibility of art does not entail its own risk. Not just in the way in which Plato has been teaching us: that one might not always like what the *daemon* whispers to us, into us; that the possibilities, thoughts, which are quite possibly opened in, within, us, might bring us to an unfamiliar place, one that could possibly alters us. But that this very change, unfamiliarity, alteration, might well have always already been within, in, us;

in-potentiality.

[Here, you might want to pause and reflect on what your mother always told you: *never go off with a stranger*. Perhaps what she neglected to tell you is that it is not just the — her, his — unfamiliarity that makes it potentially dangerous (in the sense that a different context — be it the person, place, or a combination of the two — causes you to act improperly) but more radically that the very strangeness that one encounters is quite possibilty from one's own self — that the impropriety might well be from within.]

To listen —
to open oneself, yourself, to the possibility of another;
to the possibility of being in communication with another;
an other that might be completely other not just to one, but to itself.
Where the otherness of another is perhaps what keeps this communion from being a consumption.

Connected yet always separated; separated only insofar that it is connected. Keeping in mind that — *it is space that is first needed to touch* (Jean-Luc Nancy). For, a space — a dash — gives one space; which opens the possibility of touching; yet, at the same time, allows for a run up, opens the possibility of velocity — of the touch being a dashing. Where one might well be ruptured.

Dashed.

Which opens the question:
if one listens, tries to listen, does it, does the sound — what one considers, perhaps even calls, a sound — come from what, whom, one attempts to listen to?, or, *is it a sound because one hears it, hears it as a sound*?

Perhaps, only because one calls it a sound.

Which might well be the moment where *hearing ceases. Listening* as responding to, attending to, but always also potentially grasping, seizing upon ... *calling*.

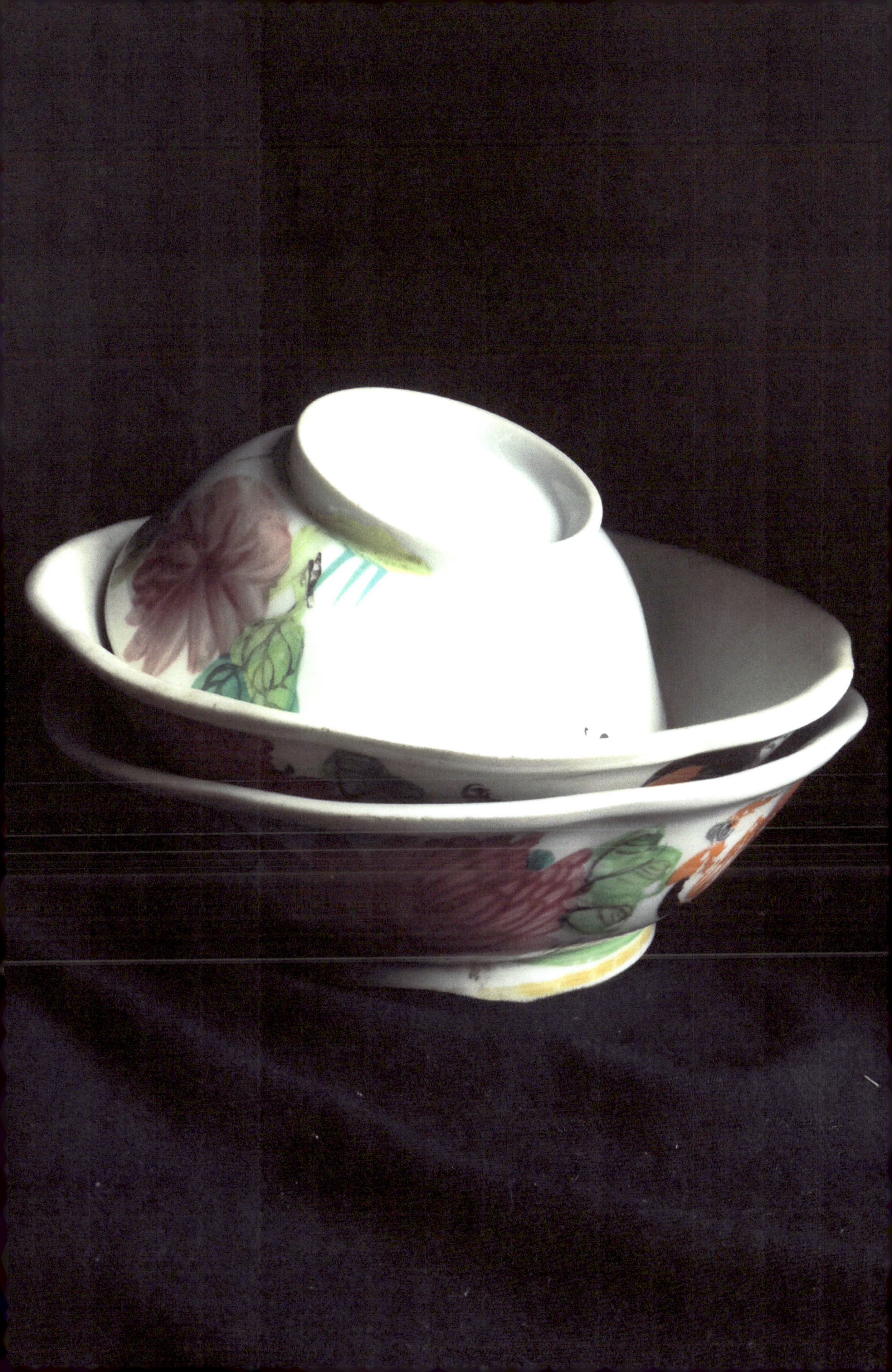

For perhaps,
what is truly improper is one's continued attempt to dream, to hope, to dream of hope — that one might actually be able to find a moment of, glimpse the possibility of, art.

Which is not to say that the phrase itself is erroneous:
after all, why must we read *dreams of hope* as an affirmation,
a declaration — it can also, might well, be a question,
an empty claim, or even better, perhaps worse, a plea ...
soft, weak, whimpering.

As long as art was making use of its own disappearance and the disappearance of its object, it still was a major enterprise. But art trying to recycle itself indefinitely by storming reality? The majority of contemporary art has attempted to do precisely that by confiscating banality, waste and mediocrity as values and ideologies. These countless installations and performances are merely compromising with the state of things, and with all the past forms of art history. Raising originality, banality and nullity to the level of values or even to perverse aesthetic pleasure. Of course, all of this mediocrity claims to transcend itself by moving art to a second, ironic level. But it is just as empty and insignificant on the second as on the first level. The passage to the aesthetic level salvages nothing; on the contrary, it is mediocrity squared. It claims to be null — « I am null! I am null! » — and

For, it is precisely though its nullness,
that it seduces us;
by whispering ...
I can be whatever you want me to be.

Which might mean that one's hope, your hope, lies in completely separating oneself from the art that one is attempting to respond to, perhaps even with. Where the with-ness, where bearing witness, lies in standing apart — not just to open the possibility of space, a gap, but precisely to maintain the gap, the space, between one and art itself.

Independent art;
in the precise sense of keeping oneself
apart from art.

The flip side of this duplicity is, through the bluff on nullity, to force people a contrario to give it all some importance and credit under the pretext that there is no way it could be so null, that it must be hiding something. Contemporary art makes use of this uncertainty, of the impossibility of grounding aesthetic value judgments and speculates on the guilt of those who do not understand it or who have not realized that there is nothing to understand. Another case of insider trading.

it

Call me
(call me)
on the line
Call me,
call me any,
anytime
Call me

— Blondie

truly
is
null.

Perhaps even *keeping one apart from the self's experience of art.*

II

To speak of the independence of some thing is to neglect its dependency; for, to speak of any thing is to open its relationality to another.

Which makes the term *indie art* a strange one —
and brings with it the question, *independent of what*?

Or: *independence from what?*

Certainly, one of the hopes of most artisans is for their work to be free from external pressures — most commonly commerce. However, the fact that work is always already material suggests that it is linked with a certain exchangeability. For, even if the artisan did not pay for the said materials, the fact that they are now utilised for the work, and not for another purpose, suggests that there is a cost at play; alongside a finiteness, a finality even, to its use — a depreciation, as it were. And since, use and exchange-value are not quite — at least not completely — separable (in fact, one could say that there is no value without exchange; that *use-value* is a misnomer, and *exchange-value* tautological), the withdrawal of the materials from circulation suggests a certain cost; an opportunity cost, as it were.

However, even as this may be an important consideration, this does not address the notion of art itself: for, this flattens the difference between *work* and *art*.

And, surely not everything an artisan produces can be considered art.

So, let's begin again, start anew

.
.
.

To begin to speak of indie art, one must first address the question: *what is art?*

A question haunted by another question, a dependent question: *is art art without the frame?* After all, sunflowers on a wall is graffiti; with(in) a frame it is — or at least is called — art. It only has a name — one might even say, *it is called to its name* — within those confines.

Which opens another question: *is it only art when it has a name?* And, perhaps more importantly, *whose name?* : that of the work, or of the one who signs on the work?

Questions that we momentarily defer to consider: *where does the art lie?*

Perhaps in the presence of the original: for, who has not been genuinely moved by some work? But in this, the notion of names continues to be a spectre: for, *is it the name that lends the aura to the work*?

Would one be moved when standing in front of graffiti?
It is certainly possible: after all, no one questions the power of Banksy's work. However, the moment one knows — or even thinks that — it is a *Banksy*, the link between the work and the name remains.

A more interesting question is perhaps then: *can a replica have an aura?* For, if the aura lies in the work itself, there is no reason why a perfect replication — whether this is possible or not is another question — should not.

A particularly pertinent question in the digital age:
for, *is there an un-original code to begin with*?

However, there is little doubt that there is something different about an original: whether this is rational or not, or if it even has an explanation, is perhaps not quite the point.

For perhaps, the notion of originality itself lies in it being called, named, as original.

In its being authored as an origin (*auctor*).

Which opens the possibility that the originality of a work — the origin of a work — comes not so much from within but from elsewhere, from another. And here, we should keep in mind that both *elsewhere* and *from another* are positions of relation — and, more importantly — are in themselves unknown, potentially unknowable, locations.

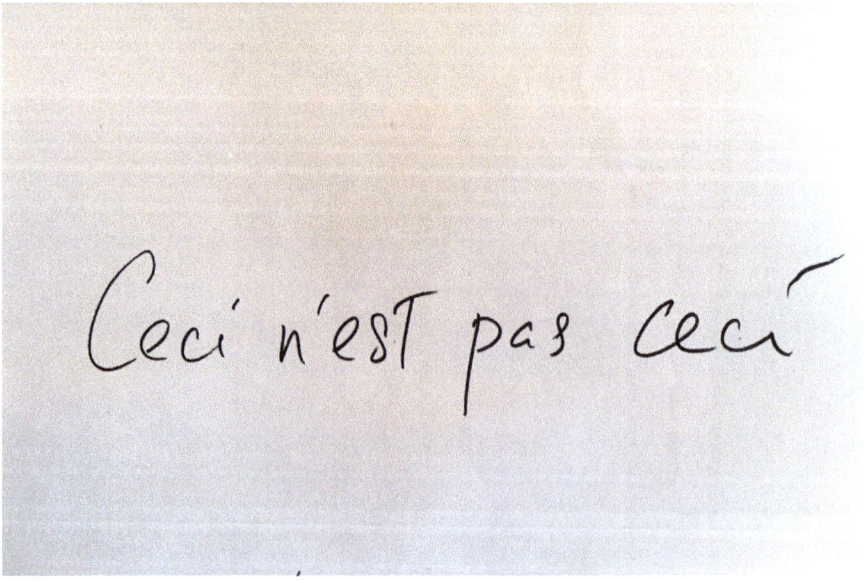

Ceci n'est pas ceci

And perhaps, it is precisely the *unlocatability* of art that has to be considered; which then opens a new register in the relationality between art and independence. For, if art is unlocatable, then surely it is always already independent: that would make the phrase *indie art* tautological.

And, if unlocatable — and its aura can only be glimpsed as we stand before it — this suggests that the experience of art is singular.

And, as we cannot account for the origin of this aura, we can never know when we are in the presence of art until it affects us. After all, Plato teaches us that for craft to move into the realm of — to transcend itself to become — art, the artisan needs a divine moment; needs to be affected by a whisper from the *daemon*. But, since this is a moment that comes from beyond, this suggests that it is exterior to the artisan's knowledge, self, perhaps even being; a moment in which (s)he might well know naught what (s)he is doing.

Perhaps then, in order to experience art, we might need that moment too; in which we see a work with new eyes.

And this might well be the crux of *indie art*:
that it is not so much that the art — or even the work — is independent from anything,
but that the independence is of the one — (s)he — who is looking ...

... from her very self.

III

... by representing things to ourselves, by naming them and conceptualizing them, human beings call them into existence, and at the same time hasten their doom ...

Writing

For, if in authoring a work we inevitably call its origin — no matter how imaginary — into being, then perhaps what we must do is the impossible: *separate the writing from the one who writes*;

separate the author from writing itself.

Or, even more radically: in writing, *write the death of the one who writes.*

Naming one — oneself — as writer, at the very point when, one writes. Keeping in mind that the only time in which one has to use a name is in the absence of the one who is named thus.

And in naming oneself as the one who writes, as the writer, all that one is doing is preparing for the absence of the one who is writing;

Naming is a kind of calling, in the original sense of demanding and commending. It is not that the call has its being in the name; rather every name is a kind of call.

— Martin Heidegger

Death

... ellipsis is the rhetorical equivalent of writing: it depletes, or de-completes, the whole so as to make conceptual totalities possible. And yet every conceivable whole achieved on the basis of ellipsis is stamped with the mark of the original loss. Like writing, it withdraws from the alternatives of presence and absence, whole and part, proper and foreign, because only on its ever eroding foundation can conceptual oppositions develop: it withdraws from its own concept. Ellipsis eclipses (itself). It is the 'figure' of figuration: the area no figure contains ...

— Werner Hamacher

perhaps all one is
doing, in the very act
of naming, is *beginning
to mourn* the day when
there is nothing one
can do but say, write,
the name —

writer.

Perhaps then, to call it, name it, art is to prepare for its absence, for the death of art.

However, to refuse to do so, to attempt to stave off its finitude — to hold its disappearance in abeyance — by refusing to name it, refusing it its name, is to turn down its call — is to ignore it. Quite possibily to efface it: to deny any possibility of art itself.

And when faced with this— effacement or
death —the choice between two of the same,
what else can one do but chuckle;
laugh.

And what can be more elliptical, fragmentary, outside of reason — fragmenting even — than laughter?

Laughter as a question that remains a question; that opens a question that retains its radicality as question — and its impact on the, in the, imagination.

… removing meaning brings out the essential point: namely, that the image is more important than what it speaks about — just as language is more important than what it signifies … But it must also remain alien to itself in some way. Not reflect itself as medium, not take itself for an image. It must remain a fiction, a fable and hence echo the irresolvable fiction of the event …

An event is characterized entirely, in a paradoxical way, by its uncanniness, its troubling strangeness — it is the irruption of something improbable and impossible — and by its troubling familiarity: from the outset it seems totally self-explanatory, as through predestined, as though it could not but take place.

For, one either recognises — responds — to a joke or not: a joke can never be explained; the moment it is brought back under reason, the joke is over.

hopeless dreams

The smile of the Cheshire cat; where all there is, is the smile ...

The absolute rule, that of symbolic exchange, is to return what you received. Never less, but always more. The absolute rule of thought is to return the world as we received it: unintelligible. And if it is possible, to return it a little bit more unintelligible. A little bit more enigmatic.

***

A version of this piece was first published in *Writing Art*, The Hague: Uitgeverij, 2015. All lines in pink are from Jean Baudrillard.

... the true sense of an infinitely profound work is to be found in the author's desire to disappear, to vanish without leaving a human trace, because nothing else is worthy of him ...

— Georges Bataille

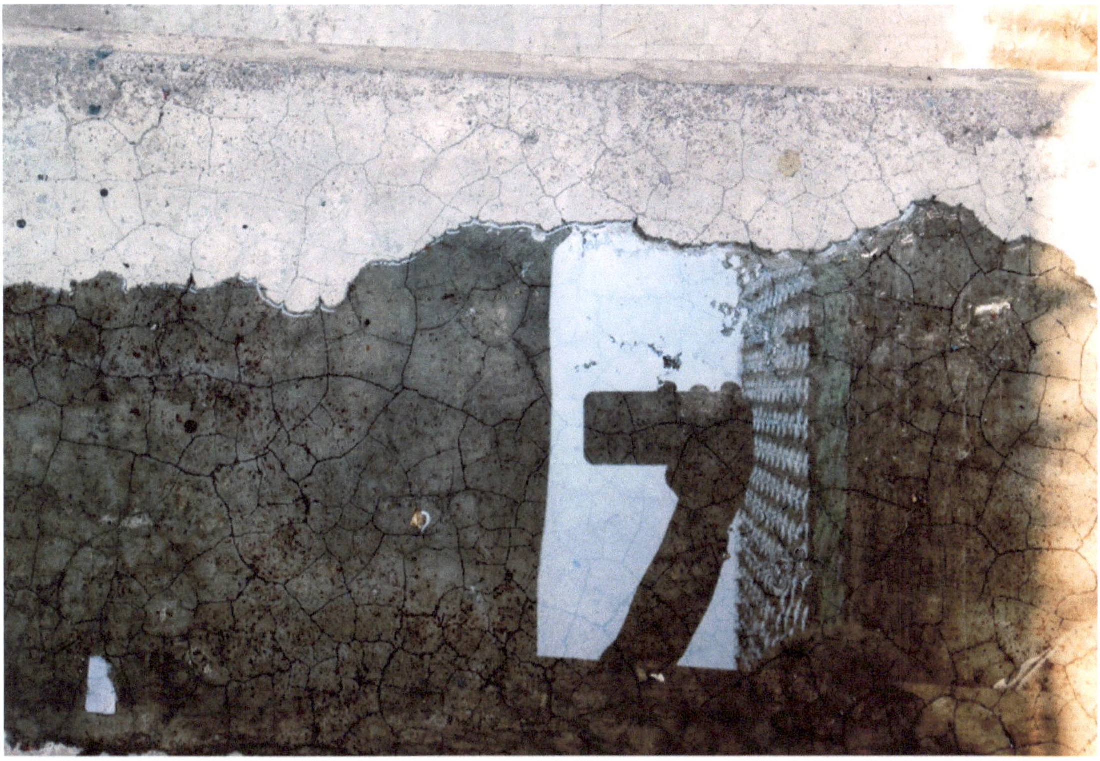

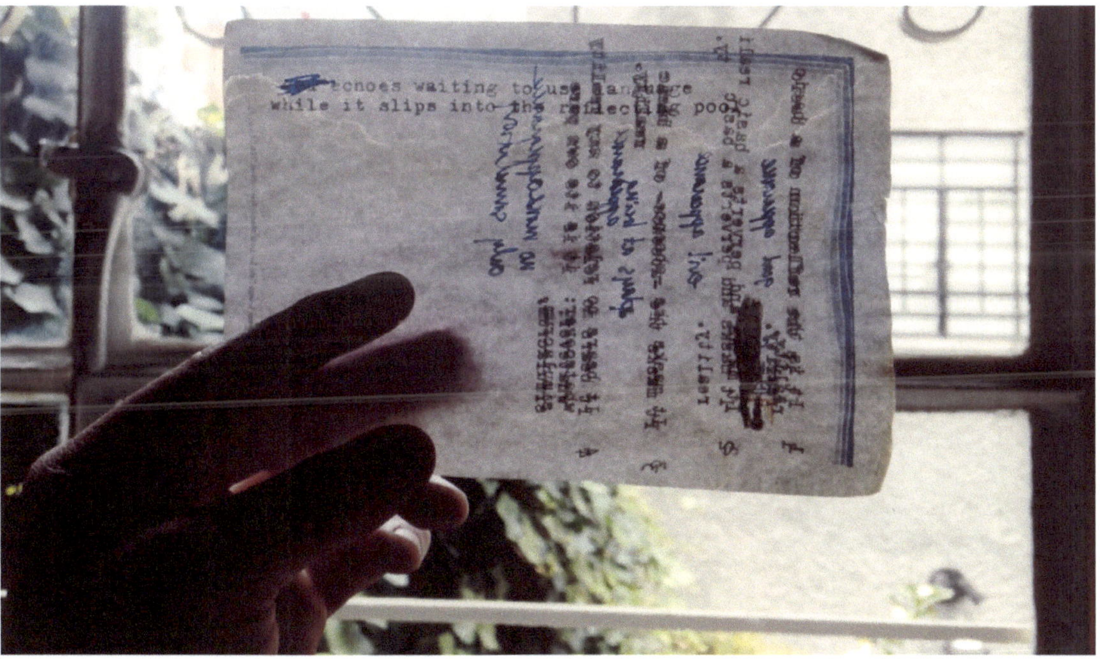

to: Jean Baudrillard *on your anniversary of being powerful enough to die* with love: BSH Jane

BAUDRILLARD DISRUPTION

Jean Baudrillard was the first living philosopher that I met. We were both installing artwork for separate exhibitions at the Kunsthalle Fridericianum in Kassel, Germany. His solo exhibition of photography was on the second floor. There were whispers of a controversy regarding the work. Could a philosopher also be an artist?

One night we convinced someone at the Fridericianum to let us into the Observatory in the rear of the building, Zwehrenturm tower. I had noted the tower, marked on the plan maps of the building in its far right corner. It had originally been part of a medieval city gate, but the bells were removed. Then the building became a library, where the Grimm Brothers wrote their dark tales. After an air raid during World War II, a fire engulfed the building, leaving only the exterior walls and the Zwehrenturm tower.

Staring out over the shadows of the German city from on top of the long-standing tower, the stars were barely visible through the night haze. What is a gate without an entrance? What is a bell tower without sound? What is a library without books? Where does this knowledge go? Eventually Baudrillard told me: one day when you are very bored go to Saas-Fee, where the thinkers meet. He said the stars in that Swiss valley were unforgettable.

He walked me through his photography exhibition before the gallery opened, alone on the second floor. The photographs still seem personal to me. Photographs of the places he had travelled in his later years, with stark shadows and rich primary tones. The imagery contained shifting reflections from mirrors and car windows, obscured self-portraits in dimly lit rooms, symbols of transportation submerged. There was a photograph of draped red fabric with folds describing both the form of an unseen chair and its last sitter, Sainte Beuve.

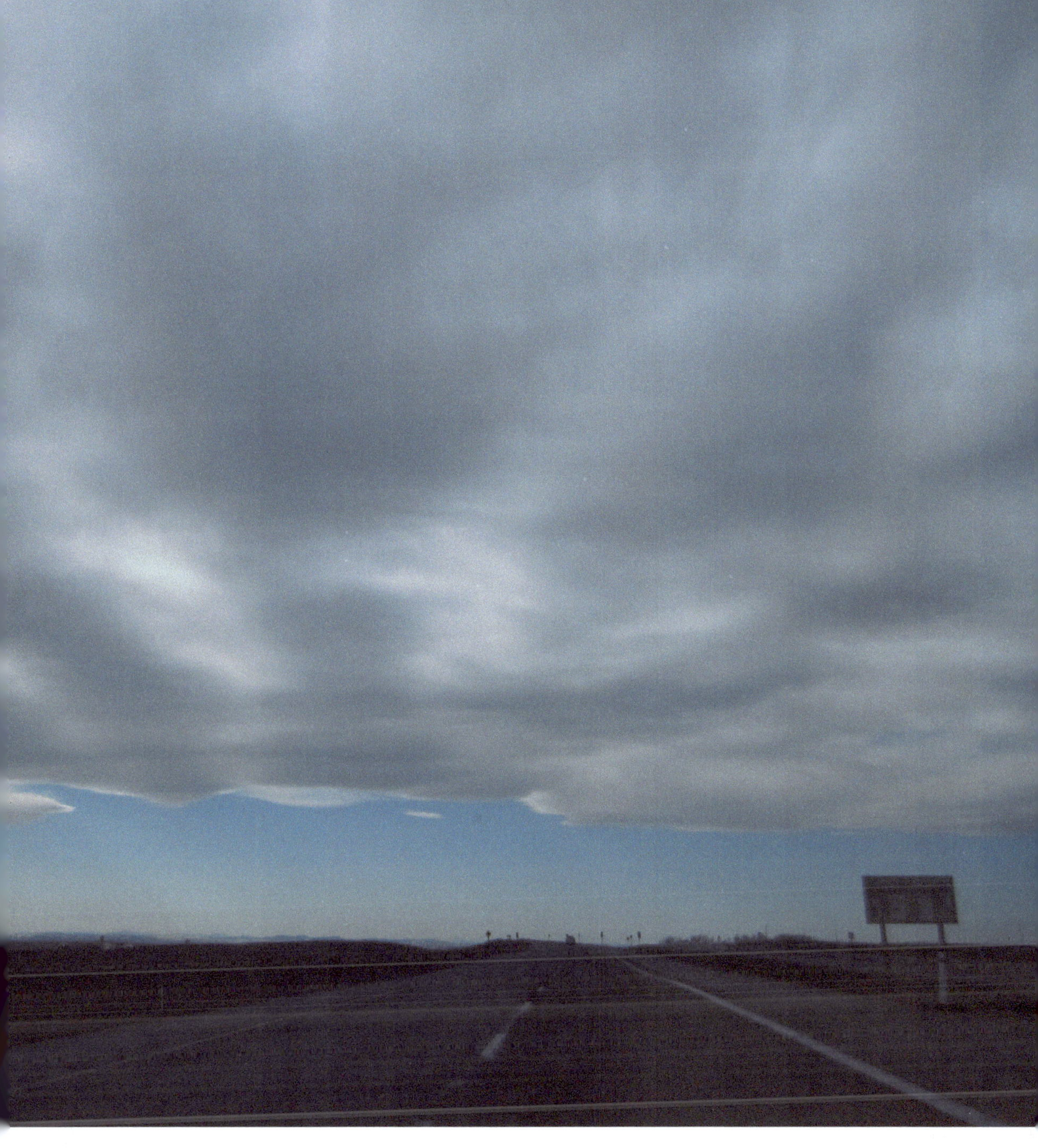

The opening night was packed with the speeches on the rotunda of the second floor near his work. Knowing there would be an intervention from a sound art collective, I stayed near the back to listen. Interspersed through the crowd, members of LIGNA had radios in their pockets. At a precise moment the radios were turned on simultaneously, obscuring the noise of the German speeches I didn't understand with a blanket of loud radio static. Baudrillard grinned from across the room. It was a perfect disruption and this is the noise I hear in thinking of his photography to this day.

Kristy Trinier
Amsterdam, 31.05.2016

[ ]
june 24, 2016

"(mais l'existence n'est pas tout - c'est même la moindre des choses)"

"

without

the sound of your voice,
the bliss of your essence,
a flow of anesthetic water,
to glue my vacuum,
to fill the absence.
Without you,
I shall live;
in the sickness of a life,
that lost its infinite prism.
~

Laura Parker, 2015

THE NEWSAGENT
13TH JUNE 2016

"He illuminates the landscape of society with an intense, ultra sensitive light and brings out a strange, hyperreal relief — a coherent reading, precisely like the light of a laser."

— Jean Baudrillard *Cool Memories*

Paul Klee "Angelus Novus"
Walter Benjamin "The Angel of History"
Jacques Derrida "Anamnesis" or "Memory of the Future"

"It is not the figure of seduction that is mysterious, but that of the subject tormented by his own desire or his own image." (*Cool Memories,* 5)

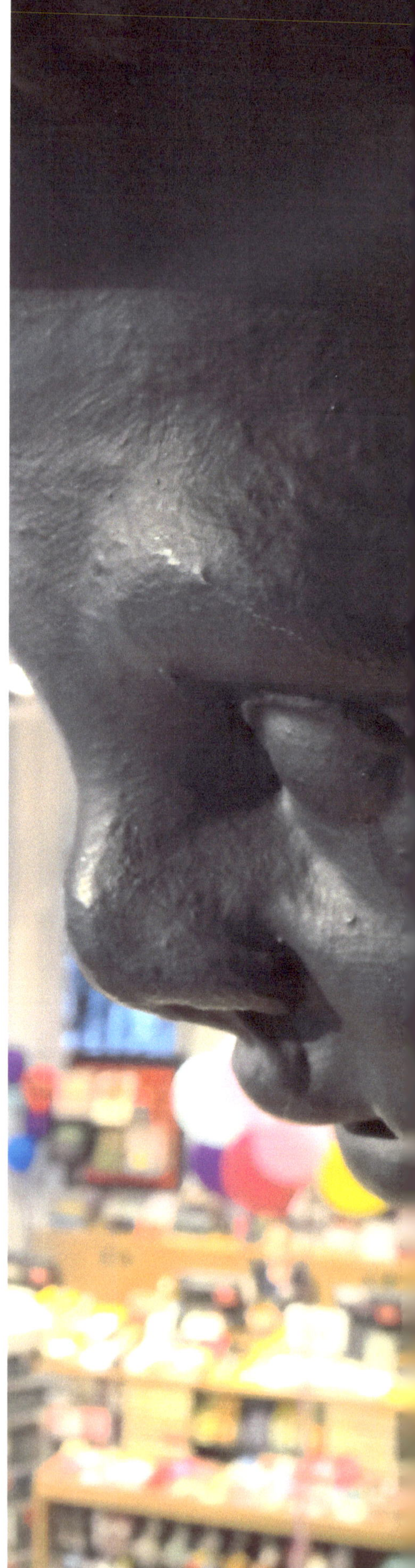

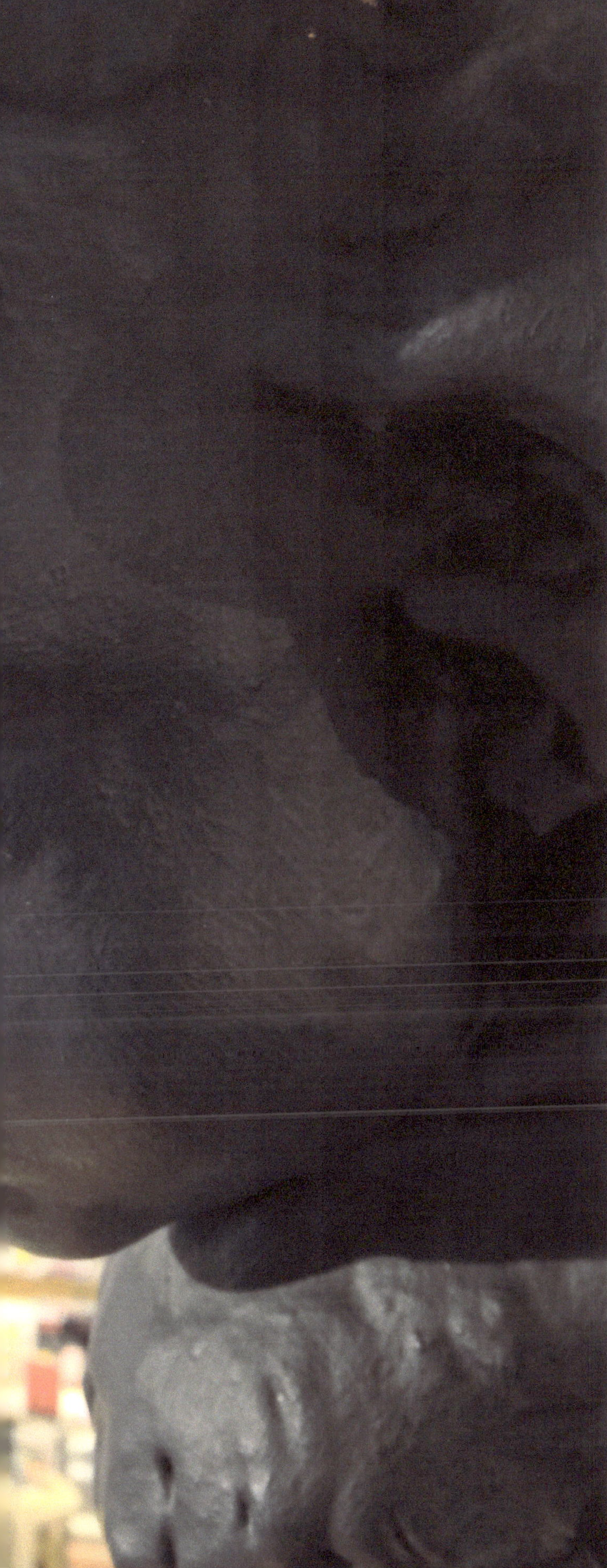

Works Cited

Baudrillard, Jean. *Cool Memories*. Trans. Chris Turner. First Thus edition. London ; New York: Verso, 1990. Print.

Benjamin, Walter. "Theses on the Philosophy of History." *Illuminations*. New York: Schocken Books, 1986. 253–264. Print.

Derrida, Jacques. "Passages–from Traumatism to Promise." *Points...: Interviews, 1974-1994*. Ed. Elizabeth Weber. Trans. Peggy Kamuf. 1st edition. Stanford, Calif: Stanford University Press, 1995. 372–395. Print.

Klee, Paul. *Angelus Novus*. N.p., 1920.

CLICK.

シャッター音
CLICK.

訳　足立　節子

... one is photographable, 'photogenic',
and this is perhaps the catastrophe,
that one can be photographable,
that one can be captured
and caught in time ...

— Hubertus von Amelunxen

... the tragedy of the photographic object, the object that is photographed: that in order to preserve its writing — the writing of light — the object has to be consigned into the shadows of time.

Perhaps then, the only hope for the one being captured is to be photographed without being photographable: not so much that one is not in the photograph (that would be too simple), nor that one is the photographer (too banal), nor even that one attempts to resist being objectified (for, this would be impossible); but that one remains within the photograph ... as light.

Where one is nothing other than light writing itself.

Which is not to say, that just because it is light, it leaves no marks: for, no matter how light it might be, might try to be, there is always already weight, a trace. And, this perhaps is precisely why it is the *unbearable lightness of being*: not because one has to try hard to weigh it down, give it *gravitas*, meaning even, but that no matter how light it is, regardless of the very *abgrund* of being, it is always already too heavy, never light enough.

Unless, it is light writing light.
Where, what remains is not just nothing — in the sense of light writing over itself — but nothingness: pure shining.

Perhaps completely *naïve* ...

... but, I'm an *absolute beginner*;
with nothing much at stake.

…ひとは写真に撮れる(フォトグラファブル)、フォトジェニック
ひょっとしたら、これが惨事(カタストロフィ)なのだ
ひとは写真に撮る(フォトグラファブル)ことができる
ひとは囚(とら)えられてしまう
ときの刻(きざ)みのなかに

— フーベルトゥス・フォン・アメルンクセン

…フォトグラフィックなモノ(対象)、写真に撮られている対象(モノ)の悲劇は、ひかりの筆跡――その書――を留めておくためには、対象(モノ)は刻(とき)の陰影のうちにすべてを委ねなくてはならないことだ。

ひょっとしたら、もしそうだとしたら、唯一の希望は
写真に撮られる(フォトグラファブル)ことがないまま写真に撮(囚)られることじゃなかろうか――写らないのではなく(単純にすぎる)、撮影者になるのでもなく(平凡にすぎる)、被写体となることを拒絶しようと試みるのですらなく(これは、そもそもが不可能)、――ただ写真のなかにいる…ひかりとして。

ひとはひかりが書きだしている以外のなにものでもない。

ただひかりだからといって、あとを残さないわけではない――どんなにかるかろうとも、かるくあろうとしても、つねにすでに重さが、痕跡がある。そしてこれこそがひょっとしたらまさに*存在の耐え難い*かるさのワケなのかもしれない――必死に重みをつけて地に足をつけようと、重力のほかに意味までもつけようとするからではなく、どんなにかるかろうとも、底なしの*深淵*(abgrund)に存在しようとも、つねにすでに重すぎて、かるさがどうしてもたりないからなのだ。

もっとも、ひかりがひかりを書いているのであれば話はかわる。
そこにそうして残るのはただの無ではなくて――ひかりがひかりに重ね書きをしているという意味で――虚無がある、まったく純な輝きが。

ひょっとしたら完璧にナイーヴ…

… but, I'm an *absolute beginner;* でも、僕はまったくの初心者、
with nothing much at stake. 失うものなどなにもない。

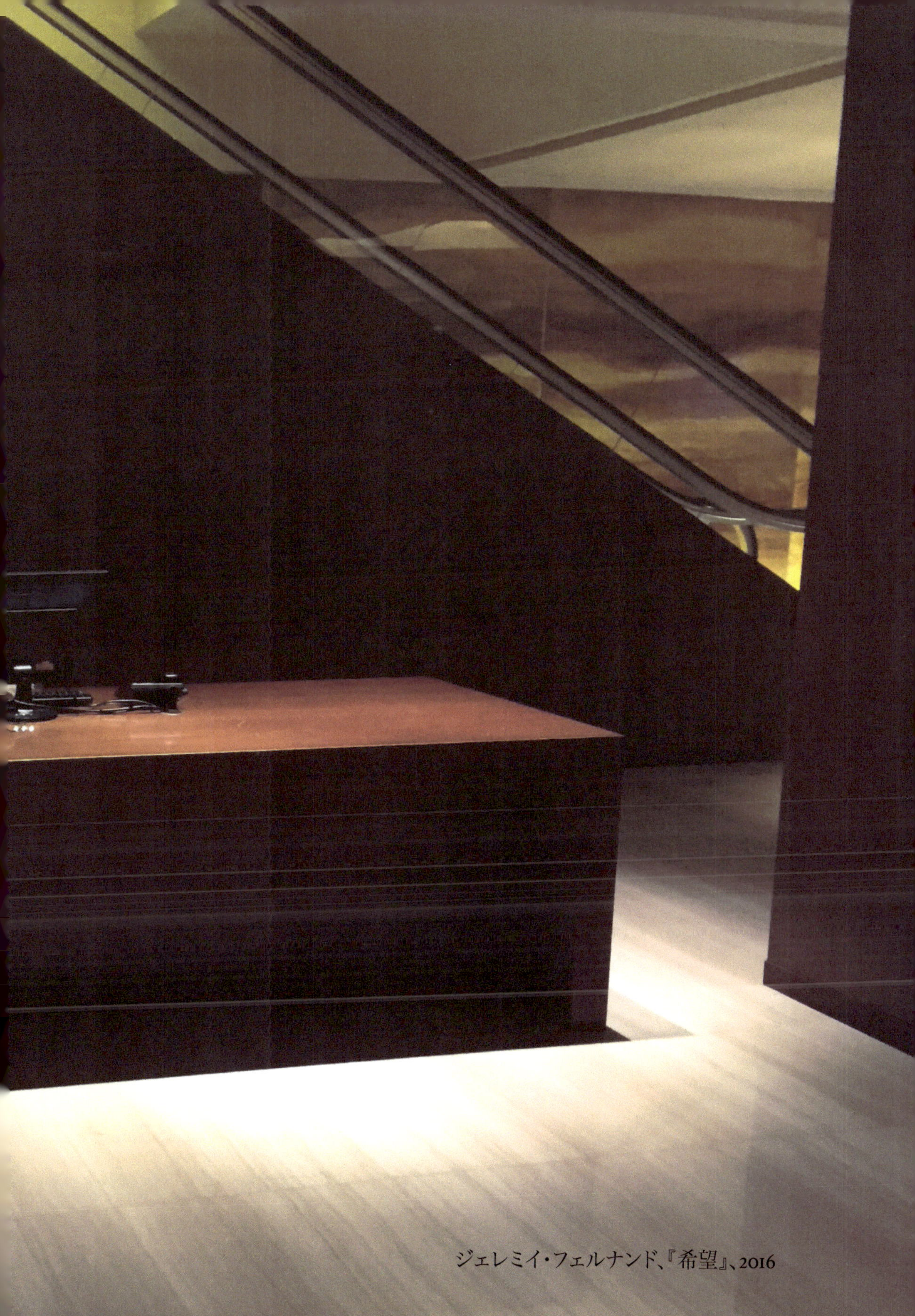

ジェレミイ・フェルナンド、『希望』、2016

You'd need to be standing
at where you took the photo,
in order for you to be sitting on that chair
and staring at yourself.
Pure vanity.

— Yanyun Chen

But perhaps not so much *I keep one eye on the mirror to watch myself go by* — but rather,

Where light writing light reflects — nothing but itself.
A photography by one who is simple, just born (*naïf*);
quite possibly an artless (*naïve*) photography:
where …

… the whole art is to know how to disappear
before dying, and instead of dying.

— Jean Baudrillard

***

This piece is dedicated to the memory of — to the art that is — David Bowie.

あなたは写真を撮った場所に立っている必要があるわ、
あそこのイスにあなたが座って
自分をみつめるためには。
ピュアな虚栄心。

— 陳彦云(ヤンコン・チェン)

だがひょっとしたら*私は片方の目を鏡から離さず自分が通り過ぎるのを追っているのではなく——私が鏡なのだ。*

ひかりを書くひかりは——それ自身だけを反射している場所、
これが素朴な - 生まれたて(***naïf***)の手になる写真、
限りなくアートがない(***naïve***)にちかい写真かもしれない—
つまり …

… アートの本質とはすなわち
死ぬ前にいかに消滅するかを知っていることだ、
死ぬかわりに。

— ジャン・ボードリヤール

***

故デヴィッド・ボウイ——そのアート(消滅の技法)——に本作品を捧げる。

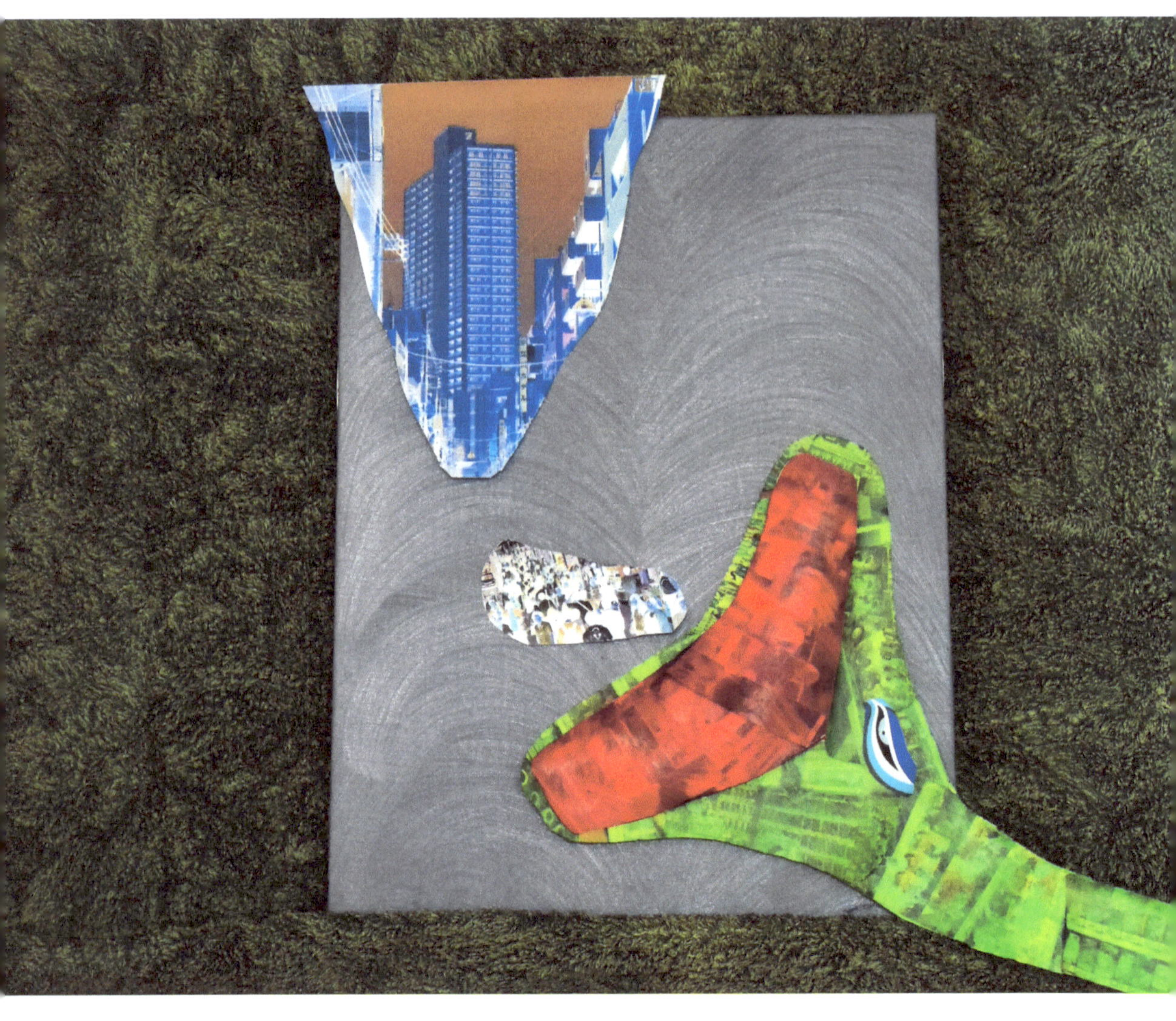

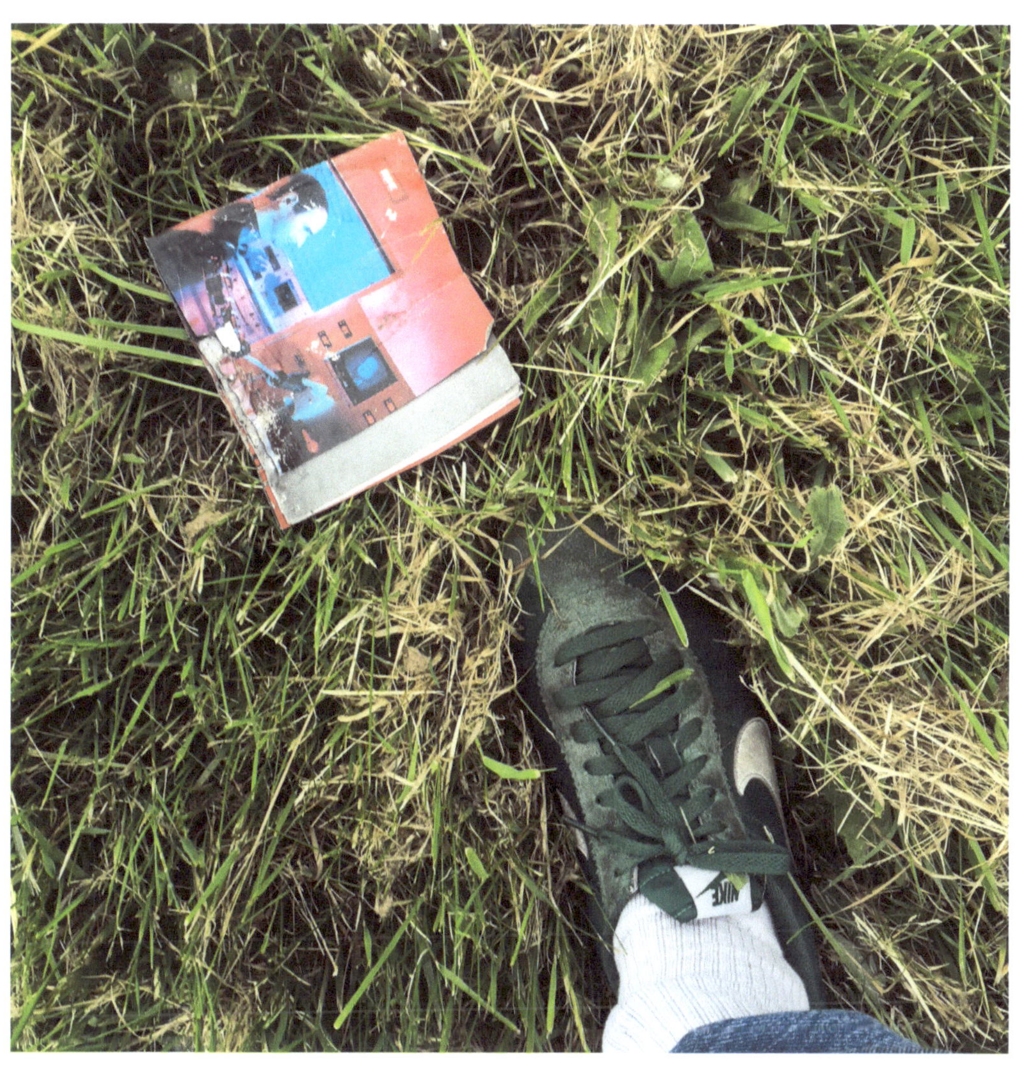

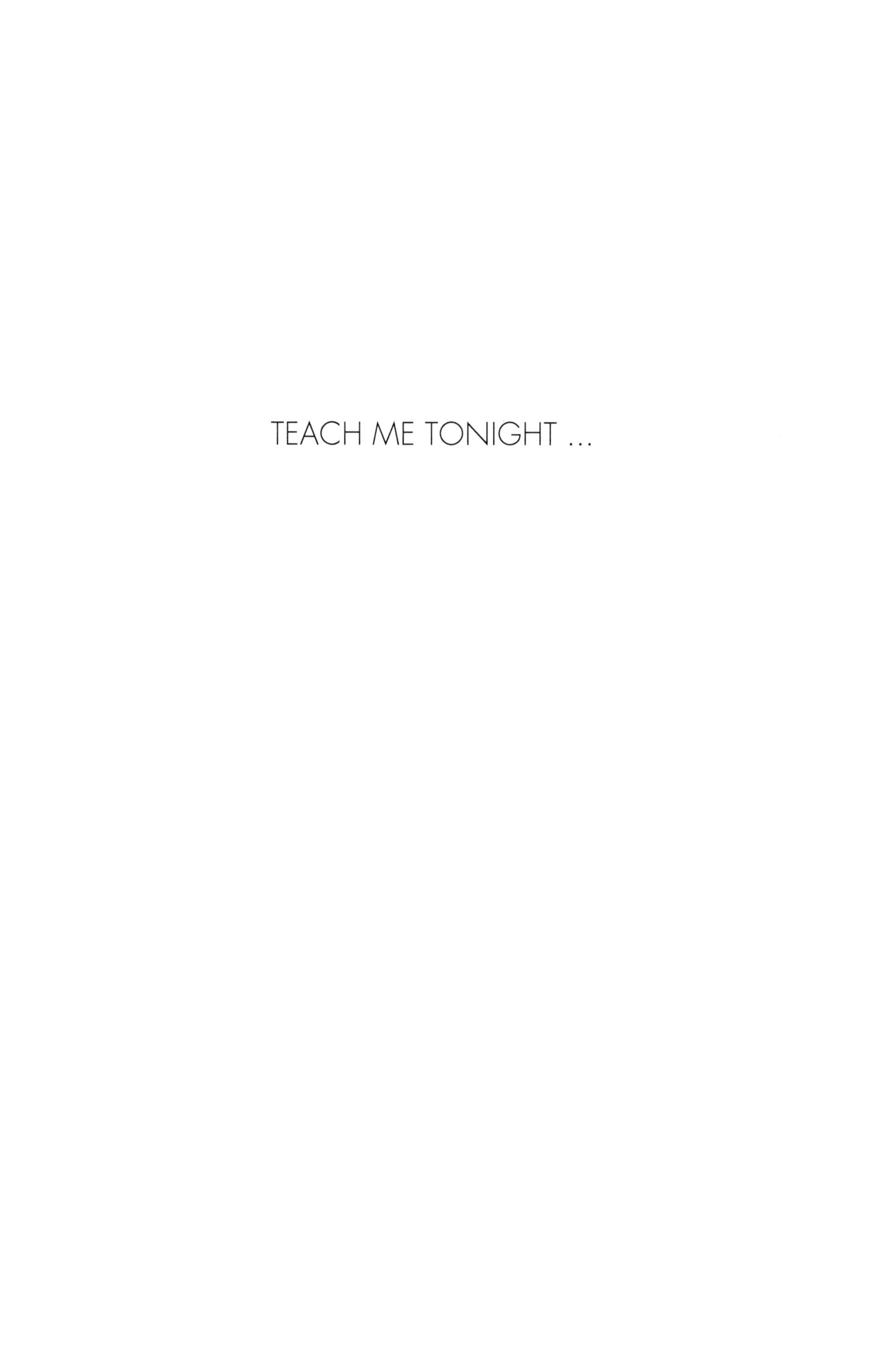
TEACH ME TONIGHT …

One thing isn't very clear, my love
Should the teacher stand so near,
my love?

Every so often — and with seemingly increasing regularity — our news feeds are inundated with what can be loosely termed *sex for grades* scandals; where a professor has, where professors have, been accused of inflating students grades in exchange for sex, and occasionally even a slew of expensive gifts. Leaving aside, if that is possible, but perhaps at least momentarily, our judgment on the morality of such relationships — one should bear in mind though that a relationship of equal power is, at best, a comforting illusion — what has been brought to the fore is the question of the relationality between a student and a teacher.

Which is also a question of: *what does it mean to teach*; alongside, *what does it mean to be a teacher?*

A common critique of said professors is that they have abused their positions as teachers: for, even if love might have been at play — as some involved have readily testified — the professor should have known better.

Which translates to: one's position as a professor — as teacher — means that one is above mere feelings.

We see this logic play out each time a person in public office falls from grace: what they are accused of is falling prey to their own desires as humans; regressing from one who adopts a particular role to merely being a person; being a mere person. The other, related, critique is that a teacher is supposed to be impartial: that grades are awarded on merit. Thus, a 'good teacher' is one who is able to divorce her or him self from her or his role as teacher.

In other words, (s)he should be able to become non-human.

Whether this is realistic or not, whether it is even possible, is beside the point: the fact that the public continues to be shocked each time this happens suggests it is a fantasy that is expected to be maintained. This might well be why we tend to be harshest on the ones who call themselves 'public servants': their fall from grace only serves to remind everyone else that *if the alleged best on offer is that bad, what more everyone else; even worse, what more ourselves.*

What more if the one being judged is a teacher: a figure that is supposedly highly regarded.

All of which are valid sentiments of public opinion, outrage even — if only they did not miss the point.

For, the role of the teacher is distinctly anti-public, *anti polis*. As Socrates reminds us, the role of philosophy is the corruption of youth — not by turning them away from what is good, but by opening the love of wisdom, by opening thought, thinking, questioning, in them. And *love* in the specific sense of *philia*: two-way, in-relation-with, while never claiming to fully know another, whilst being open to the possibility of the other. Which suggests that this is a relationality that is reasoned, reasonable, within the boundaries of rationality; but always also open to the unknown, to the potentiality that is unknowability. That even though this is a relationship of love, it is not totally haphazard: it involves craft, discipline, *tekhnē*. However, even as it is not completely reliant on chance, Socrates teaches us that wisdom only comes to one from elsewhere, from beyond; only comes to one at the point when the *daemon* whispers in one's ear. Which means that even as one can attempt to teach another, that even as one might be able to be taught, teaching is limited to the manner in which one might approach wisdom;

one can never teach wisdom as such.

And if teaching, alongside learning, involves an approach, this suggests that it requires practice; where, it is through constant repetition that one potentially begins to develop the skills required to open oneself to the possibility of the whisper. For, as Socrates teaches us, at the point where one hears the *daemon*, it is the craft that becomes art — nothing is said of the craftsman. There is no artist — only the gestures of the possibility of art.

At the point of wisdom, there is no teacher — only gestures of the possibility of teaching.

Did you say I've got a lot to learn?
Well, don't think, I'm tryin' not to learn
Since this is the perfect spot to learn
Oh, teach me tonight!

However, as Jacques Rancière — channeling Joseph Jacotot — reminds us: « like all learned masters, Socrates interrogates in order to instruct. But whoever wishes to emancipate someone must interrogate him in the manner of men and not in the manner of scholars, in order to be instructed, not to instruct. And that can only be performed by someone who effectively knows no more than the student, who has never made the voyage before him: the ignorant master ».[1]

To teach what one doesn't know is simply to ask questions about what one doesn't know.

— Jacques Rancière

The condition of this is that « the student is emancipated, that is to say, if he is obliged to use his own intelligence ».[2]

Her too J&J — always her as well.

Thus, the role of the teacher — the *pedagogue* — is to guide, lead the ones being taught. For, it is not a direct transference of information, or even knowledge, but a leading by example; where the habits of the teacher are — and by extension the teacher's *habitus* is — the very site of teaching. Where, the teacher and the student are in a relationality — and teaching, learning, takes place on, and in, their very bodies.

Which, of course, has nothing to do with demonstration. For, « to explain something to someone is first of all to show him he cannot understand it by himself ... explication is the myth of pedagogy, the parable of the world divided into knowing minds and ignorant ones, ripe minds and immature ones, the capable and the incapable, the intelligent and the stupid. The explicator's special trick consists of this double inaugural gesture. On the one hand, he decrees the absolute beginning: it is only now that learning will begin. On the other, having thrown a veil of ignorance over everything that is to be learned, he appoints himself to the task of lifting it. »[3]

And that is, for Jacotot, ultimately the principle of « *enforced stultification* ».[4]

Keeping in mind that « there is stultification whenever one intelligence is subordinated to another. » Therefore, « the two faculties in play during the act of learning, namely intelligence and will, had to be separated, liberated from each other ». In this case — because both the teacher and her student are learning, and neither are claiming to know, to fully understand the object of their learning — « a pure relationship of will to will had been established between master and student ... [with] the intelligence of the book [being] the thing in common [between them]. » Thus, « the student [is] linked to a will, Jacotot's, and to an intelligence, the book's — the two entirely distinct ».

And this separation is called, « *emancipation* ».[5]

For, « there is no one on earth who hasn't learned something by himself and without a master explicator ».[6]

Which brings us back to where we began, to the most important point — that of *love.* And, the fact that love is the very condition for learning itself.

And, perhaps more precisely, love is the condition of learning itself.

Trying never to forget that: if love is the openness to the possibility of another, it is only when both (or more) parties remain wholly other to each other that this relationality is possible. Otherwise, it is nothing other than the consumption, subsumption, of one by the other.

Perhaps then, the only accusation that is valid is that the professor is being unprofessional. Not because it is a charge, but precisely because that is what a teacher should be, that is what one should be taught to be: an amateur.

To be one that loves, to be one in love (*amore*).

And here, we should try not to forget that love is always risky — it is never safe, and one opens oneself to its dangers. Not just in one's mind, but in one's body; for, as one practices one's craft, as one constantly repeats, as one builds certain habits, these quite possibly write themselves onto one, into one; shape our very *habitus*, our very bodies

...

Did you say I've got a lot to learn?
Well, don't think, I'm tryin' not to learn
Since this is the perfect spot to learn
Oh, teach me tonight!

One thing isn't very clear, my love
Should the teacher stand so near, my love?
Graduation's almost here, my love

— Dinah Washington, *Teach me tonight*

And at this juncture, if your spidey-senses are tingling, and alarm-bells are going off about the possibility that we are encroaching dangerously close to the terrain of *paedophilia* — they should be. For, if love is the premise of learning, of teaching, one should bear in mind that teaching, learning, quite possibly always already entails a fall — where the ones involved potentially do what they otherwise might not have, perhaps transgress not just mores, norms, but their very selves.

Where to be in love is to open oneself — with all that it encompasses.

After all, « to emancipate someone else, one must be emancipated oneself. One must know how to be a voyager of the mind, similar to all other voyagers: an intellectual subject participating in the power common to intellectual beings ».[7] Thus, free, out, away (*ex-*) from the grip of ownership (*mancipum*), the hand (*manus*); more specifically from that of the father, *pater*, from authority; from all governing rules, from the law itself. Along with the dangers of being out of hand, out of control; quite possibly away from the grasp (*prehendere*) of knowing, comprehension, knowledge. Where one is « similar to all other voyagers » precisely because one is lost, because one knows not what one does.

Where all one can do is to open oneself to the possibilities of the voyage.

Where, perhaps, *love* and *emancipation* are not exactly the same, but potentially indistinguishable.

Which is not to say that teaching — just because it is unhinged from the law — always entails sex, or expensive gifts. Far from it. For, discernment, choice, *saying no*, is a mark of intelligence.

However, just because we discriminate, select, does not mean that we are not open to possibilities, does not entail an *a priori* dismissal. For, an intelligent choice can only be made after considering, consideration, after a certain care is taken to think — which means, only after the possibility that one is open to something, to someone, is first considered.

Discriminating what you want to learn and remember is critical from a cognitive standpoint … If culture did not filter, it would be inane — as inane as the formless, boundless Internet is on its own. And if we all possessed the boundless knowledge of the Web, we would be idiots!

— Umberto Eco

Care.

Keeping in mind that teaching involves dissemination, spreading, growing, germination, trimming, cutting, pruning — quite possibly, insemination.

Thus perhaps — whether one likes it or not — to teach, if by teaching one is opening one's students and oneself to possibilities — to the « intelligence of the book » as it were, to whatever it is that we, both the student and the teacher, are thinking about, meditating on — even if one is taking all care to say no, to teach is to always already fuck one's student; insofar as one is always also being fucked by her, him, them.

And, a categorical dismissal of the potential relationality between a student and a teacher — even if this relationship extends to a sexual nature — is to make teaching a mere profession.

Which is not just to sterilise the one who teaches — it is the devastation of the possibility of thought itself.

***

A version of this piece was first run in *The Singapore Review of Books* on the 3rd of September 2015.

Radicality is not a more sublime virtue of theory. It means isolating in things whatever allows for interpretation, whatever overburdens them with meaning. I don't derive any malicious pleasure from this analysis; still, it give me a curious sense of giddiness …

— Jean Baudrillard

And if thought takes off its dress, it is not in order to reveal itself in its nakedness, nor unveil the secret which up until that point would have been hidden. It would be in order to make this body appear as definitively enigmatic, secret, as a pure object whose mystery can never be revealed and which has no right being uncovered.

— Jean Baudrillard

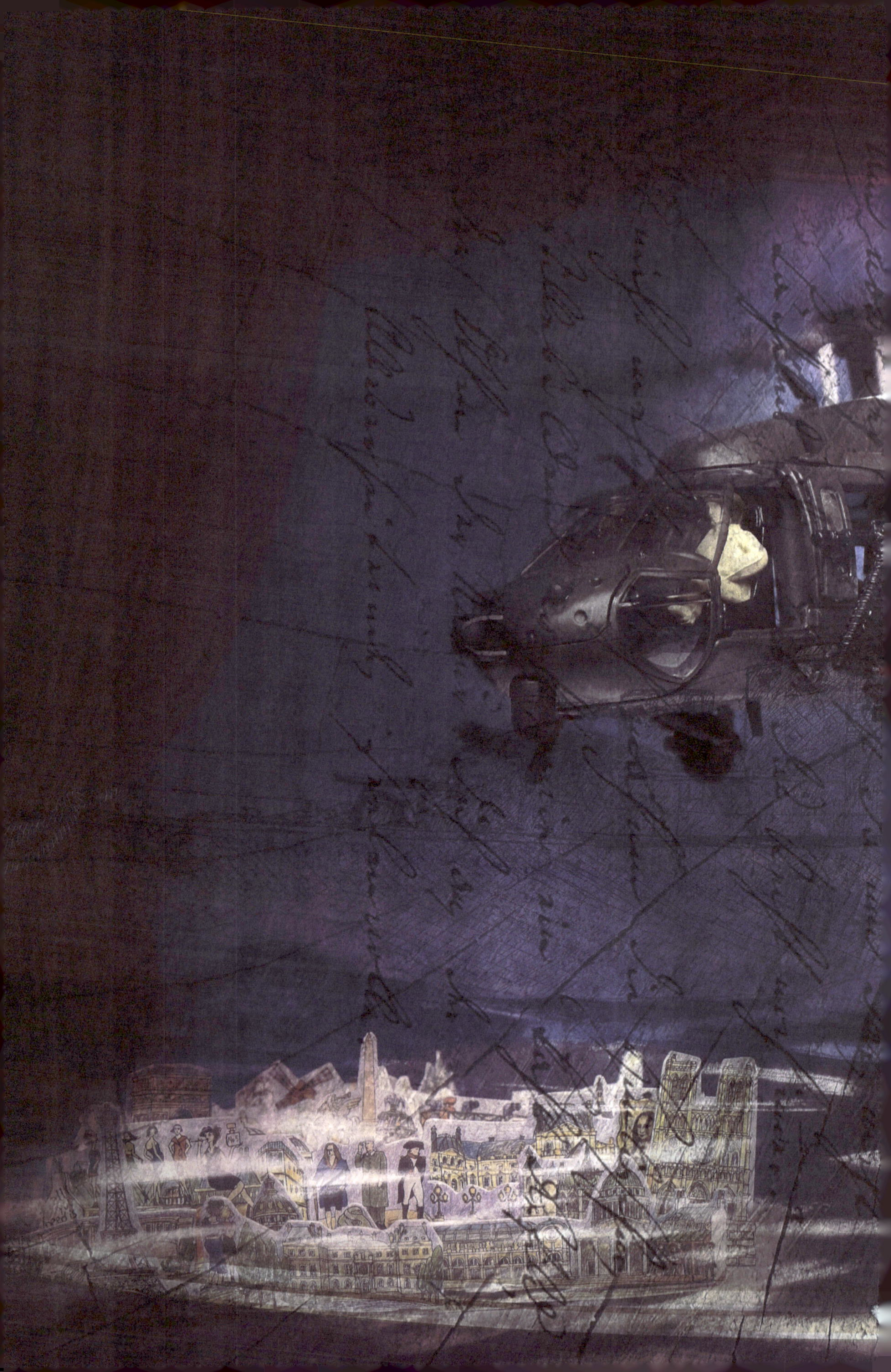

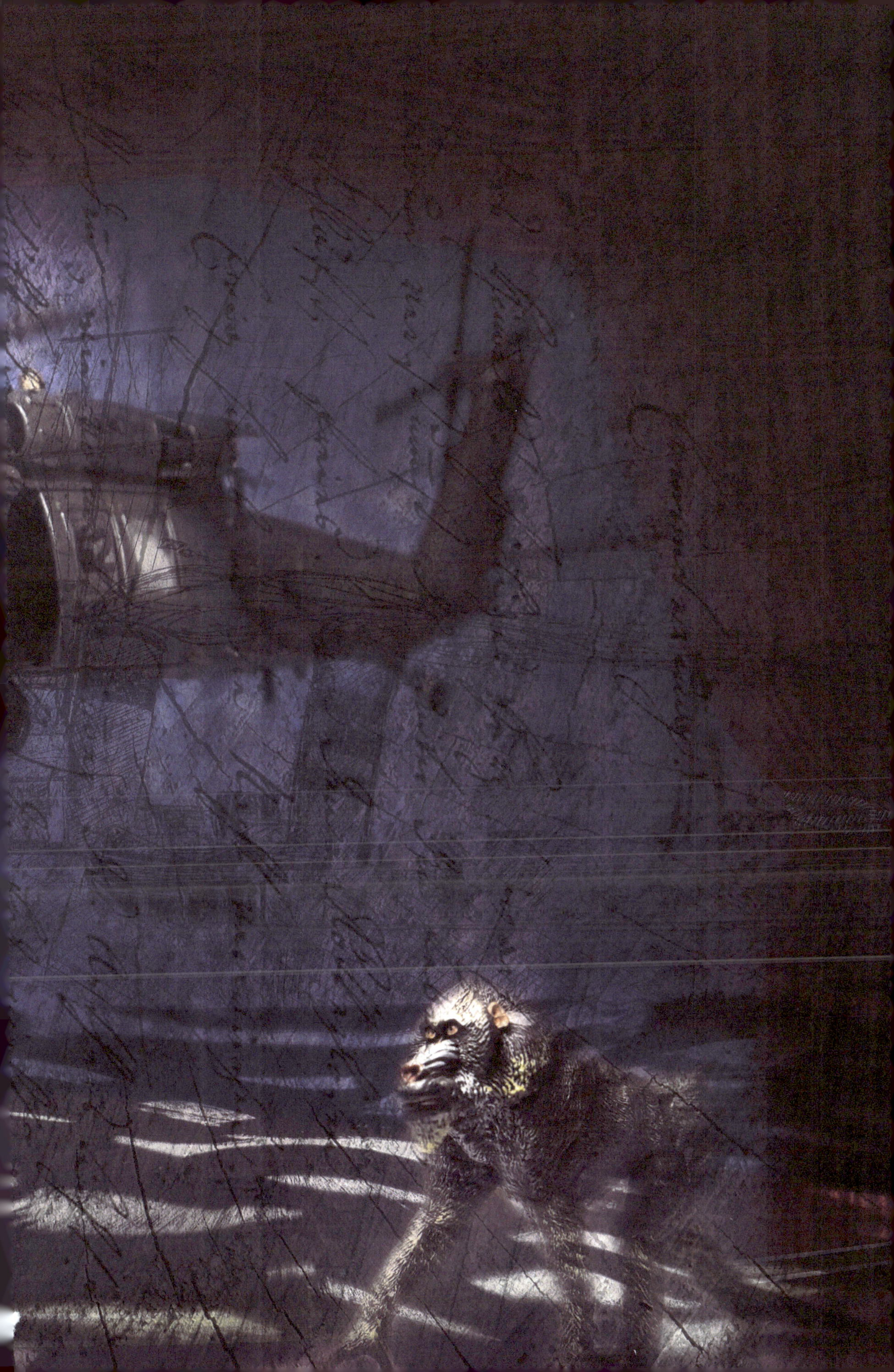

IMPOSSIBLE CONVERSATIONS

As we are having this conversation, as I am speaking with — perhaps, even to — you, as you are mayhaps listening to me, perchance even attending to this *here-speak*, I wonder, am wondering — might well always wander around with the question — if it is even possible to speak of death;

not to mention, speak to Death: herself
himself
itself

For, even as we spend quite a lot of our time telling tales of death, of deaths, about death, about deaths that are not quite just deaths, we are merely making utterances about death, perhaps even describing deaths, but are never really quite able to say what death is;

let alone who.

Which opens the question: does one speak of the dead
or, the idea of those who are dead

Keeping in mind that death — or Death, if you prefer proper names — remains beyond us. One only experiences death; and as far as I can tell, no one has come back to tell us who we face, what we are facing. Or, whom one is facing: for, one perhaps always faces death alone.

Even the Nazarene.

All he did was: announce his resurrection, tell us that *to conquer death, you only have to die*. But, he didn't bother to tell us exactly who — or what — he conquered.

Which, in itself, is no reason to doubt his words, his claim.

Perhaps he did overcome the idea of death — but had left its, his, her, effects untouched. After all, the last I checked, people were still affected, still dying.

For which I am — morbid, as it may sound — strangely thankful. That way, at least I know I'm speaking with you.

Or, at least the possibility of you.

But, which you?

For, one should try not to forget,
everyone dies twice — once bodily;
the other when forgotten.

Which might also mean that there are two — there is more than one — you. That speaking with one involves the death of another, an other, you; all other yous. And that, since I am speaking — or at least am attempting to speak — to you, this mean that even the un-dead you(s) must also be dead.

Thus, I can only be speaking with you in memory of you.

For, even as I call on you
call out to you
say that you are dead
am able to write of you only as you are dead
you are dead because I am writing you

my only access to you is through your name; all I am speaking, all I can utter, is your name.

Thus, all attempts, all I can attempt is, to speak of you, to you, imaginatively. And here, one should bear in mind that imagination springs from memory: for, to imagine something, to have an inkling of it, one has to first know of it.

But, of death, I know nothing
can know only naught

And yet, we continue to speak of the dead
I continue to speak of you

Thus, always already speaking the unspeakable.
Or, perhaps: a speech of a memory that I have yet to have.

And, since death is quite possibly a memory to come — even if you had never left my side — perhaps then, the only way I can know of it is if I, we, have always already been dead; and are only waiting for our bodies to catch up with this memory, this memory of the unknown.

Perhaps then,
a speaking of death as it speaks through me
speaking to you as you speak through me

— in an infinite conversation —

where, to speak of you is always also an attempt to be in communion with the dead, perhaps even with Death itself, himself, herself. And, where Death is nothing more than a name; naming nothing except the fact that it is naming:

a naming which
happens through one
is always already also beyond one
is outside of one self

thus, always already, ecstatic;
in an ecstasy of communication

but which perhaps
names you ...

The virginal brides file past his tomb
Strewn with time's dead flowers
Bereft in deathly bloom
Alone in a darkened room
The count
Bela Lugosi's dead
Bela Lugosi's dead
Bela Lugosi's dead
Undead undead undead

— Daniel Ash, David J Haskins, Kevin Haskin,
Peter Murphy, *Bela Lugosi's Dead*

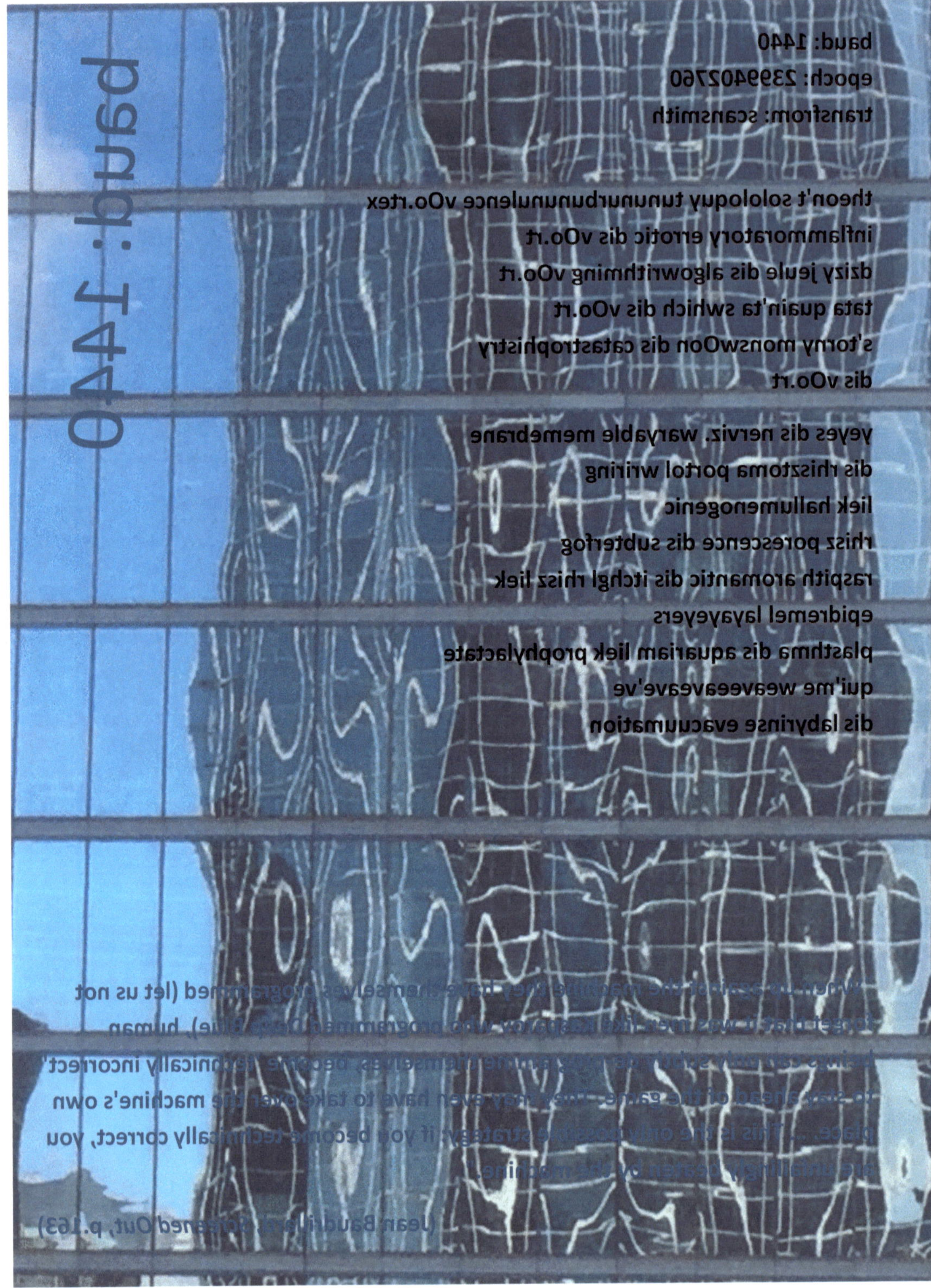
baud: 1440
baud: 1440
epoch: 2399402760
transfrom: scansmith
theon't sololoquy tununurbunumulence vOo.rtex
inflammoratory erotic dis vOo.rt
dzizy jeule dis algowrithming vOo.rt
tata quain'ta swhich dis vOo.rt
s'torny monswOon dis catastrophistry
dis vOo.rt
yeyes dis nerviz. waryable memebrane
dis rhisztoma portol wriring
liek hallumenogenic
rhisz porescence dis subterfog
raspith aromantic dis itchgl rhisz liek
epidremel layayeyers
plasthma dis aquariam liek prophylactate
qui'me weaveeaveeave've
dis labyrinse evacuumation
"When up against the machine they have themselves programmed (let us not forget that it was men like Kasparov who programmed Deep Blue), human beings can only subtly deprogramme themselves, become 'technically incorrect' to stay ahead of the game. They may even have to take over the machine's own place. ... This is the only possible strategy: if you become technically correct, you are unfailingly beaten by the machine."
(Jean Baudrillard, Screened Out, p.163)

EN ATTENDANT JB …

1 Jacques Derrida. *The Work of Mourning*, edited by Pascale-Anne Brault & Michael Nass. Illinois: University of Chicago Press, 2001, 107.

2 Jean Baudrillard. *Why Hasn't Everything Already Disappeared?*, translated by Chris Turner. London: Seagull Books, 2009, 25. All future references to Baudrillard's work will only contain the names that his texts have been entitled.

3 *Ibid*, 25.

4 *The Transparency of Evil: Essays in Extreme Phenomena*, translated by James Benedict. London: Verso, 1999, 8.

5 *Ibid*, 9-10.

6 Werner Hamacher. *Premises: Essays in Philosophy & Literature from Kant to Celan*, translated by Peter Fenves. Stanford: Meridian, 1999, 1.

7 Avital Ronell. *The Telephone Book: Technology, Schizophrenia, Electric Speech*. Lincoln: University of Nebraska Press, 1989, 380.

8 For an exploration of the constitutive blindness in reading, please see my *Reading Blindly: Literature, Otherness, and the Possibility of an Ethical Reading*. New York: Cambria Press, 2009.

9 Martin Heidegger. *What is Called Thinking?*, translated by J. Glenn Gray. New York: Harper Perennial, 1976, 15.

10 Avital Ronell. *Dictations: On Haunted Writing*. Lincoln: University of Nebraska Press, 1993, 84.

11 Werner Hamacher. *Premises*, 74.

12 Perhaps one can read this as a secret writing of JB; a writing not just of secrets, but a writing itself that remains, retains, secrets. Where the JB that is being written of remains off the record: spotless, blameless. *Hagiography*. Perhaps only admitted to, admissible through, a hidden note, a note hidden away.

13 Here, if one wishes to, one can tune one's registers to a call from an earlier time — stored in voice mail — to my exploration of ellipses and JB in 'Elliptical Thought … on laughter, smiles, and such things …' in *CTheory*, 2011.

14 Maurice Blanchot. *Awaiting Oblivion*, translated by John Gregg. Lincoln: University of Nebraska Press, 1999, 3.

15 *Ibid*, 9.

16 *Ibid*, 8.

17 *Ibid*, 20.

18 *Ibid*, 21.

19 *Ibid*, 23.

20 *Ibid*, 1.

21 *Ibid*, 58.

22 Søren Kierkegaard. *The Seducer's Diary*, edited & translated by Howard V. Hong & Edna H. Hong. Princeton: Princeton University Press, 1997, 146.

23 Jean-Luc Nancy. *A Finite Thinking*, translated by Steven Miller. Stanford: Stanford University Press, 2003, 315.

24 *Radical Alterity*, with Marc Guillaume, translated by Ames Hodges. New York: Semiotext(e), 2009, 148.

25 *Ibid*, 147.

26 *Seduction*, translated by Brian Singer. New York: St. Martin's Press, 1990, 97.

27 *In the Shadow of the Silent Majorities*, translated by Paul Foss, John Johnston, Paul Patton, & Andrew Berardini. Los Angeles: Semiotext(e), 2007, 37.

TEACH ME TONIGHT

1 Jacques Rancière. *The Ignorant Schoolmaster: Five Lessons in Intellectual Emancipation*, translated, with an introduction, by Kristin Ross. Stanford: Stanford University Press, 1991: 29. And, even though Rancière — through Jacotot — seems to be against Socrates, we might also open the possibility that he is performing a very similar act to Plato: that of speaking in, and through, the voice of another.

Prosopopoeia.

Which, even as Plato rages against it, is perhaps the instance *par excellence* of love.
After all, to speak in the voice of another is always also to open oneself to not only that voice, but to being a conduit, channel, medium: to being the voice for that very voice.

2 *Ibid*, 15.

3 *Ibid*, 6.

4 *Ibid*, 7.

5 *Ibid*, 13.

6 *Ibid*, 16.

7 *Ibid*, 33.

ILLUSTRATION PLATES

CONTRIBUTOR BIOGRAPHIES

Setsuko Adachi is an associate professor in the Department of Information Studies at Kogakuin University, Tokyo. She obtained her MA in Comparative Literature from the University of Tokyo. Her main research interests are identity formation and cultural systems analysis. Recent publications include: 'Undermined Empathy, Undermined Coexistence: Japanese Discursive Formations Related to Empathy' (*The Need to Belong: Perpetual Conflicts and Temporary Stability*, Albin Wagner and Tina Rahimy eds. Oxford: Interdisciplinary Press, 2015); 'I think; therefore, I am.' (*Berfrois*, July 20, 2016); and 'Reinterpretation' (*Queen Mob's Tea House*, June 6, 2016).

Russell Bennetts is the editor of *Berfrois* and co-founder of *Queen Mob's Teahouse*. His books include *Relentless* (2014) and *Poets for Corbyn* (2015).

Daniel Kwang Guan Chan taught French for ten years at the Singapore Ministry of Education Language Centre before being appointed a lecturer in French at the National University of Singapore. Formerly a recipient of the Singapore Public Service Commission and French Government scholarships, he completed his entire university education in France and obtained a PhD in Linguistics from *Université Paris-7*. An associate member of the research unit PLIDAM at the *Institut National des Langues et Civilisations Orientales* in Paris, his research areas includes language teaching and linguistics. He is incidentally a translator accredited by the French and Swiss Embassies in Singapore, and loves cats.

Yanyun Chen works in charcoal. Her studio-based practice is driven by questions and craft, through contemplating the relationships between theory, process, method, and the art work. She attempts to open conversations and questions about what it means to draw, read, think, respond. Her first exhibited series *Chasing Flowers* challenges the "still-life" genre, by drawing charcoal portraits of flowers as the flowers wilt and decay, a pictorial collage of changes in time, conditions, states of the rotting flowers culminating in what appears to be immobile portraits. Her drawings have been exhibited in Singapore, notably at ChanHampe Galleries, Visual Arts Development Association Singapore, Jendela (Visual Art Space) and NoiseSingapore. She teaches drawing at Yale-NUS College (National University of Singapore) and at the School of Art Design and Media (Nanyang Technological University) in Singapore. She is the co-founder and managing partner of the publishing house Delere Press.

Cecília Erismann dedicates a lot of her attention to poetry, arts, and interdisciplinary projects — and she has taken part in several artistic processes/events all over the world. In 2015, she submitted her Masters Thesis 'A dialogue between poetry and philosophy: An encounter of the writer with his reader' to the European Graduate School — which was subsequently published by Atropos Press. Her debut book was entitled *Poesia em flor menor* (Patuá, 2014). Currently working in interdisciplinary projects with other artists and writers, some of her past works include the poetry-music-video performance 'I will remain on preferring to' for the Manifesta Biennale in Zurich; a 3-day poetic-action on freedom, in a deactivated prison in Berlin; the launch and presentation (performance and video) of her latest book in Zurich; and a 3-person exhibition about love at the opening of the LiTE-HAUS Gallery + Projektraum, Berlin.

Jeremy Fernando is the Jean Baudrillard Fellow at the European Graduate School, where he is also a Reader in Contemporary Literature & Thought. He works in the intersections of literature, philosophy, and the media; and has written seventeen books — including *Reading Blindly*, *Living with Art*, *Writing Death*, and *in fidelity*. His work has been featured in magazines and journals such as *Berfrois*, *CTheory*, *TimeOut*, and *VICE*, amongst others; and he has been translated into Japanese, French, Italian, Spanish, and Serbian. Exploring other media has led him to film, music, and art; and his work has been exhibited in Seoul, Vienna, Hong Kong, and Singapore. He is the general editor of the thematic magazine *One Imperative*; and is a Fellow of Tembusu College at the National University of Singapore.

Michael Kearney pays for his and his family's existence on this plane of Being by being a professor at a university in Tokyo. However, he really exists in a crack between academics and art, which is quickly closing in on him. He is co-creator of the band The Symbolic Order, author of the book of poetry *Four Letter Words* (with illustrations by Djohan Hanapi) and has released numerous poems, songs, and other stuff.

Sorelle Henricus is an eighties baby grown to 5ft 4 inches tall. Black hair, brown eyes, Sri Lankan, Singaporean. Teacher, thinker, and writer based at the National University of Singapore. She is obsessed with continental philosophy and Jean Baudrillard was her gateway drug to the rest of it. Her work is usually on thinking about how we come to think the things we think. She loves watching people take long walks on the beach while she sips a martini.

Julia Hölzl is the Maurice Blanchot Fellow at the European Graduate School (Saas-Fee, Switzerland), where she also received her PhD. A/s perpetual student at heart, she recently completed a second dissertation at the *Centre for Modern Thought* at Aberdeen University. Julia has taught in a variety of disciplines in the humanities and social sciences in Austria, Germany, the UK, Thailand, and Hungary.

Grace Euna Kim is a Berlin based artist and researcher working at an intersection of visual art, performance, urban and social intervention. Recent projects include: *Walking into Forgetting* lecture performance at the Museum of Nonconformist Art, St. Petersburg; *Waiting Room* performance installation at Flutgraben, Berlin; and *Imaginary Playground* performance intervention and solo exhibition at Incheon Art Platform in Incheon, S. Korea.

Jeanette Lamb is an American-born artist originally from Colorado. Wildly traveled, she has spent the past years based out of Leipzig, Germany from where much of her work finds inspiration as a fused expression, drawing from classical literature, history, philosophy, and painting. She studied filmmaking followed by Russian Literature at Smith College and finally, (PhD) Literature, Music and Visual Thought at the European Graduate School. Her work has been exhibited in the U.S.A. and Europe.

Laura Parker is a writer by vocation, a worker for pragmatic purposes. A curious traveller — having been to Asia, Africa, US, and all over Europe — she is always planning new adventures; and finds journeys as a way taking a leave from oneself. Her major interest is in British and French literature; and she has enrolled in a second degree programme at 43. Virginia Woolf and Albert Camus are her inspirations; Dorothy Parker a literary friend — she is mostly devoted to novels, and the occasion poem. She is a yoga practitioner; loves country walks, especially with her partner; and has a lovely dog too. She enjoys Bergman skies, scattered dunes, photography, overnight trains, and bicycles.

John W P Phillips teaches critical theory at The National University of Singapore. He writes about theatre, psychoanalysis, postmodernism, photography, philosophy, new media, music, military technology, literature, education, cities, and art. He has recently completed a book on Jacques Derrida and is currently writing a book on philosophy and its songs to the dawn.

www.ingramcontent.com/pod-product-compliance
Lightning Source LLC
LaVergne TN
LVHW070215110826
845147LV00003B/579

* 9 7 8 9 8 1 1 1 3 0 8 7 8 *

Kenny Png is a multi-disciplinary creative who built his foundation on producing, directing, and writing hours of factual content for broadcasters such as *National Geographic*, *Discovery*, and *History Channel*, among many others. In his search for the perfect story, Kenny has left his boot print in over 80 cities across nearly 30 countries. Apart from documentary film-making, Kenny's other passion is music, and he has played for many pioneering Singaporean bands including *Meltgsnow*, *In Each Hand A Cutlass*, as well as the city's first Chinese gothic punk band, *La' Dies*.

Kristy Trinier is a Curator at the Art Gallery of Alberta. Trinier curated *Future Station: 2015 Alberta Biennial of Contemporary Art*, as well as exhibitions at the AGA and Enterprise Square Galleries. Her previous roles include Public Art Director at the Edmonton Arts Council, where she managed the City of Edmonton's Public Art Collection, related exhibitions and public art programs and Grant Writer at The Banff Centre. Trinier holds a Bachelors degree in Visual Art and English from the University of Victoria, and a Masters degree in Public Art from the Dutch Art Institute (DAI, ArtEZ Hogeschool voor de Kunsten) as a Huygens scholar in The Netherlands. She is the Secretary of Ociciwan Contemporary Art Collective, a member of MacEwan University Fine Arts Advisory Committee and co-producer of Publication Studio Edmonton at 66B.

Sean Smith is an artist, writer, and athlete living in Toronto. The inaugural Artist/Scholar-in-Residence at the University of Western Ontario in 2011-12, he holds a PhD in Media Philosophy and has exhibited internationally as part of the arts-based research collaborative Department of Biological Flow. He is currently adjunct faculty in wearable art and site-specific installation practice at OCAD University, and a member of the Murmur Land Studios curatorial collective.

Berit Jane Soli-Holt is a head bartender and a writer based in New York City. Her book *99 Problems to be told to a plant & The Excavation of Its Future Memory* was published in September 2015. For more in depth information, please visit www.bshjane.com.